FOR MY FATHER AND MY SON

I would like to express my thanks to the people of Shetland who gave me invaluable support while writing this novel in the form of a grant from the Shetland Islands Council, and to all the others who helped in other ways, especially my wife Wilma.

Glimmerwick is a fictitious community which I have imagined to lie somewhere along the coast to the north of Hamnavoe in Northmavine, near Tingon. All characters are imaginary.

ROBERT ALAN JAMIESON,
18th September 1985.

PART ONE: INTRODUCTIONS

LERWICK RHYTHM

When I was a boy the town breathed with a special rhythm
The early morning blow of the St. Clair steamer
Tuesdays Fridays
The opening rumble of grey metal steamer's store doors
Knots of eight o'clock dockers
A seine netter low in the harbour water
Mottled white with gulls
A special rhythm.

Saturdays was a bag of 9d chips from Albert's at ten or eleven
Sucking pockets of vinegar from the bottom corners
(Ma wondering about nibbled Saturday dinners)
A 1d fishing line from Goudie's or Jimmy Irvine's
A game of football in a road or street
Not twenty or fifteen but ten years ago
A special rhythm.

Now the Greenhead's flattened, fashioned
For the oil age pulling at the chords of the rhythm.
But we never played there anyway.
And Albert's, Goudie's and Jimmy Irvine's have gone.
(Try playing football under the wheels of cars and lorries)
Lerwick's rhythm has quickened.
But the St. Clair still blows, Tuesdays and Fridays
And gulls still mottle seine netters in
A special rhythm.

ROBBIE ROBERTSON (1976)

New Beats New Rhythms

The latest in the line of steamers to bear the title M.V. *St. Clair* does not berth at Victoria Pier in the heart of the old town of Lerwick, as its predecessors did. This new roll-on-roll-off link with the south rests in the special terminal built for it in the new dockland areas to the north. The old steamer store which straddles the bulk of the old pier is no longer abuzz, twice a week. Now its empty shell is silent concrete and steel, a graveyard of Lerwick's past, when the ferry lay cosy in the womb of the town.

There is a new Lerwick rhythm — or rather a number of different beats, occasionally in time but often clashing — a cacophony of oil age sounds.

There are strange faces on the winding main street, where once faces were familiar. New influences have penetrated through its skin of northern tradition. The pace of shore front life has quickened — the town has grown. There is less time to stop and talk, less time to exchange smiles, less time to think.

But come with me, see the changes for yourself. Come with me to a small café on Commercial Street, overlooking the harbour swell.

Sip your coffee, glance outside. See how the old flagstones have been replaced by concrete cast in a mould. Commercial Street's quaint architecture has been moulded too, into a strange symmetry where shops which sold everything in true emporium fashion have been superseded by specialist establishments, meeting the new technological needs. Even in this café, the evidence is present — waitresses bring well-packaged goods, produce of another culture — what did you expect, blaand and kirn milk, reestit mutton and baps? These ancient delicacies belong in another age — this change cannot be resisted.

Just beyond the pierhead, at the Market Cross, people pass by hurrying. Overhead, seagulls swoop and dive in the high winds. In the harbour, the fishing fleet has assembled to wait out the forecasted storm; boats of many nationalities crowd together, sheltered by the old pier, like a flock of sheep behind a stone dyke. The crewmen crowd into shorefront bars to play darts and pool. Alehouse spirits lift as bottles empty, beer bellies protrude from under heavy jumpers, beards grow on unwashed faces. The smell of the sea and of fish fills the air, to mingle in with smoke and curses and brawling laughter. Pint glasses overflow onto tiled floors, lino collects dirt on the sticky surfaces of missed mouthfuls.

It is a November day in Lerwick. In Bressay Sound beyond the harbour walls, the sea chops white frothy teeth into a grey blue swell. Among the buildings of the old town set on the slope above, grey figures run through a biting rain shower. Cars weave round tight corners, speckled with drops of water half fresh from the gloom above, half salt from the ocean spray.

Lowrie a'Wurlie, a crofting man from the north of the islands, moves along the narrow main street, wearing a heavy overcoat covering his only suit. On his head he wears his best flat cap. Today he has sold his wool clip to the Lerwick broker. He carries two plastic bags from the Co-op full of tins of beer and whisky bottles. He has received a better price than in previous years.

"Man," mused Lowrie to the smiling broker, "dir wis a time when du got nothin for dy oo. But noo it's aa changed."

Commercial Street is burgeoning with Fair Isle knits for the tourists. In the crofthoose and cooncilhoose homes, fingers flicker as the soft yarn thread jumps the broomstick of the needle, over and over and over. The pattern grows. But more and more, the rasp of machines is heard above the click of the needles. The old silent way is impractical, unable to compete with the oriental manufacturers.

Light fades fast in the afternoon. Suddenly the street lights are all around, reflecting in a yellow glare from the rain-soaked tarmac. Schoolchildren appear from hidden classrooms, to drittle idly along Commercial Street in the half dark. Boots splash in puddles, fluorescent armbands light up in beams from car headlamps.

Lowrie a'Wurlie waits for the bus home. He buys a poke of chips from the Viking Café and reads the month-old news on the scrap of newspaper, the *Aberdeen Press and Journal*. He spots a report on lamb sales at the city marts, but the prices fetched are wrapping someone else's chips.

At half-past three the bus departs for the north, pulling slowly up the hill away from the town. Lowrie looks northwards, and through the mirk he sees the distinctive glow of the main gas flare at Sullom Voe Oil Terminal. The bus radio plays away the long miles through the Lang Kames, where a deserted moorland valley skirts the new oil age highway north. Then to the west, the sea glints blue and the village of Voe is reached. Lowrie winces as he looks on the estates of new houses which have been built there. To his mind they are depressing in their uniformity, all lit up with lights in identical windows. The bus continues on along the side of a sea loch till it reaches Brae, another village afflicted by this oily sprawl. When Lowrie was a young man, courting, he went many a night to dances in the hall there. Now the Brae that Lowrie knew is lost, swallowed up and gone.

The two-lane highway ends a few miles further north and transforms into the old single-track road, winding its way along the shores of a series of small, peaty hill lochs. Then it climbs to the top of a brae and there, to the east, between the hills, lies Sulom Voe, the huge urban outpost, the oil terminal. It makes a striking spectacle, vivid and alive in the mirk of the night like a downtown area of some lost city — a myriad lights shine out of the gloom, surrounded on all sides by blankness and above all shines its beacon, the gas flare.

To Lowrie a'Wurlie it is a gigantic alien, constructed out of nothing natural by hands which never belonged to faces.

Soon the bus reaches its terminus at Hillswick, where the crofter's van is parked outside the pub. He takes his carrier bags and heads across the pierhead, as the gale gusts about him. He throws his purchases into the van with relief and closes the door. The vehicle splutters into life, and he pilots it carefully out of Hillswick, lighting a roll-up as he goes while holding the steering wheel between his elbows. Miles wind by, tight corner after tight corner. He passes the odd lonely crofthouse set against the moorland's folds. Finally the lights of Glimmerwick appear, at the crest of a small hill, and the van rolls home to rest.

Glimmerwick: five houses in a kind of horseshoe, where the road ends in an ultimate tarmac full stop. Below lies the sheltered anchorage which has given its name to the settlement, a small cleft in a wall of red sandstone.

Glimmerwick: it is the kind of place which you might drive to, turn your car and leave again, untouched by the world inside its houses. This would be easily done. There would be no impression made, save that of ultimate isolation.

Yet these houses have life inside them, laid upon the ghosts of many others. They reach back into the past with clawed hands, mirror in microcosm the Shetland of today and the promise of its future. There is a story here, which if not told, will follow its characters to their graves, buried on a windy Tuesday like this, in a silent kirkyard where seabirds swoop low and squawk.

THE MAN IN THE LANE

Running up the steep hill above the shore in Lerwick, above the Esplanade and Commercial Street, are a number of thin lanes as old and full of secrets as the winding main street itself. Their names are stories from an earlier era, but stories lost — Pirate Lane, Navy Lane, Hangcliff Lane — timeless links with the past. Not so many years ago, this area of the town was its slums. The houses perched on the hillside were old and damp — and finally empty. In recent years, many of these dwellings have been refurbished and folk have created fine new homes within the walls of the old.

It was here the Linda lived the first four years of her life, in a small house behind the main street bakery, halfway up the lane.

Her mother filled the house with flowering plants — peonies, fuschias, pelargoniums — wherever there was a flat surface free she set a pot. She had a strong love of green life and yearned for a real garden, but that being denied her, she focused her attention on the house plants and they responded. They grew tall and straight stemmed, and bloomed in abundance.

Linda remembered a red geranium that stood on the ledge of the window above the kitchen sink. She remembered how the petals would fall, lie scattered for days, as brilliantly red as they had been attached to the mother plant, as if reluctant to surrender their beauty. She remembered how much they looked to her like drops of blood.

Her father was a fisherman. She couldn't recall him clearly, only his smell in the house, fishy, salty and alien. She thought she could picture his face leaning over her bed at night, huge and fleshy lipped, smiling through a beard. She thought it was his face but couldn't be sure — it resembled photographs she had seen of him since.

His boat put into a sheltered voe in the north of the islands in view of a gale warning on the wireless. It seemed the safest thing to do. He was on deck with another man, gutting the catch, as the boat rolled in the heavy swell. Overhead, an angry sky was breeding heavy clouds that whisked from north to south, casting down squally showers as they passed. When the wave hit the boat, breaking huge and fearsome over the bows of the craft, it carried him over and buried him deep. A frantic search revealed nothing.

Days later, his ugly swollen body washed ashore on the pebbly beach of a neighbouring island. It was the risk they took. Every year there was tragedy. Prayers were pointless.

Linda could recall the day he was lost. She remembered the open door of the house, the awful wailing sound that snaked its way out, the slow steady stream of people who were close, and their heavy-faced condolence.

She was very frightened. She couldn't understand. The mood of the house changed. Formerly healthy plants drooped through lack of care, the atmosphere became sullen and thick.

She would lie awake at night and listen to the sound of the storms. In between the whistling gales and the thrashing rain, she would hear the almost inaudible sobs coming from her mother's room. There was no wailing after that first day. But for Linda, those tiny sobs, secretly cried, were worse. Those sobs were present in her most terrifying nightmares. Those, and the man in the lane.

She had no idea, looking back, why she should have become so scared of this innocuous person as a small child. Perhaps it was that she knew him without knowing him, that he walked through her dreams in the middle of the night. Whatever, she woke at the sound of his footstep every night that he passed. That tiptoeing, almost lilting step, as if he were trying not to wake her, as if he were trying to sneak around to avoid detection.

Slip-slap, his feet on the stone steps outside, as he passed by the house on his way down the steep lane. Slip-slap, drifting off into the night without trace.

Like her father, lost in the night. Except that the man in the lane came back, every night, without fail. Every night of the week: but not weekends.

This was the clue which led her to deduce his mission, much later in her life. Of course, he was a baker, on his way to work when the rest of the town was asleep. Of course he was. Yet in her childish terror, he was a ghoul, a being of another dimension, sent to torment her nightly.

And in the little house behind the bakery, where the smells of fresh-baked bread were as much a part of morning as waking up, she quaked in her sudden chilled bed as he passed.

She was well used to this tyranny by the time she finally saw his face. That night, as she peeked from her bedroom window shivering with fear, he looked up and the sight of his eyes, cold and vacant and half shut, compounded her terror into something still worse. Now there was a picture vivid in her mind to match the slip-slap of his footsteps, and pierce through her paltry defences so powerfully that she saw it even if she closed her eyes and hid beneath her blankets.

Of course he was a baker on his way to work, every day of the week except Saturdays and Sundays. Of course he was. Yet even in the far-off days of rational thought and womanhood, the face returned in her dreams, the symbol of everything unknown and threatening.

Her mother became thin and drawn in the months following her father's death. She'd been a healthy, vigorous woman, with heavy build and full breasts, almost six foot tall. As her weight dropped, so she seemed to stoop, until her neck looked as if it began below her shoulders and the whole of her upper torso sloped forward in an ungainly manner.

Truth was, even the most basic tasks such as feeding herself and her child became an almighty struggle for her. She was so shattered by her husband's untimely end, so shocked, that she didn't even print a note of thanks in the local paper to the folk who'd taken up a collection for her and the child.

So shocked that the neighbours began to discuss her state quite openly, sometimes even in the same room as the distressed woman, who appeared not to hear.

But Linda heard. They thought she was only a child and didn't understand, which was true to an extent, but she knew they were talking about her mother, and she saw the expressions which twisted their faces as they spoke. Their voices were full of pity, but there was another mood present too. It was something Linda didn't recognise, but she knew intuitively it was bad. Sometimes she would catch a sentence or two of their talk which would bore into her pride like a power drill till it burst and anger poured out.

No one liked the child. She had such fits of temper. Even if you felt sorry for her, you still couldn't bring yourself to like her. She was frightening to behold, screaming and shouting, tugging at the hand of her hollow-faced mother, her hair long and wild, hanging in her face. And that temper! Who could ever know what lay behind such behaviour?

Linda knew. She knew in an instinctive way which forced realisation whether she wanted it or not. Like the face of the man in the lane which came to her nightly, no matter how hard she tried to shut it out.

The water used to run like a river down the narrow lane when it rained. The ancient planners had made little provision for site drainage. Linda, four years old, in a red coat that was far too small for her, stood in the steep lane trying to block the flow of the water. Neighbours peeped out of lace-curtained windows. The rain beat the town till it was awash. They frowned. What was the child doing out in such weather? The lass would catch a chill.

Linda was trying to force the elementary law of gravity to take a beating. For centuries, the rainwater had run down the lane in a rush, following the same route, gushing over the steps in tiny waterfalls, running smooth over the less inclined stretches, till it reached the main street below and there dispersed into a flat shallow loch barely moving. For years it had followed these patterns, till the stone steps showed signs of delicate erosion.

And there in the very worst of the storm, in the steep slope above the bakery, a tiny girl in a sodden red coat stood determined to dam the river with whatever material she could find. She grew angry when her foundless attempts were washed away. But then, she wasn't to know that nature must finally take its course.

As activity in the house behind the bakery became more and more estranged from convention, the pity that the widow had at

16

first smothered in changed form. The odd things that happened there, the cries in the middle of the night, her weird conversation, it all became too embarrassing. Besides, the woman no longer took proper care of her child.

Finally, some nameless do-gooder contacted the distraught widow's sister. She lived in the north of the islands, had recently married there. After all, she was the only family left. She had to take some responsibility.

The events of the next few weeks scratched deep into the consciousness of the child. Everything that had composed life for her, all the basic elements that were present in the compound of her existence at that time, were suddenly removed, erased like graphite from paper, leaving her marked with their imprint.

Gone the house in the lane, gone the spectre who had walked through her dreams, gone the familiar structure of the town around her, the appetising smells from the nearby bakery, gone her tall kind smiling mother.

Her aunt, Clemmie, told her that her mother was going away for a while. That she was resting. That she was ill. That she, her aunt, would look after her till her mother was better.

It was a fine spring morning, the air full of sea fog, but fresh on her cheeks. Clemmie turned the key in the lock, and took her niece's hand. Together they walked up the steep lane to the Hillhead, where Clemmie's husband was waiting in his Austin A40. Linda carried her own small suitcase. She refused to give it up to her aunt. In it, she had her clothes and her tattered teddy bear. She looked back over her shoulder at the house above the bakery, where she had lain silent in her bed, afraid of the night and its mysteries.

Inside the house, the furniture remained. But the wardrobes were empty and the beds had been stripped of their linen. In the kitchen, in the window over the sink, a final red petal dropped from a dying geranium. It landed in the cracked sink and as the water dripped from the tap, it was carried fraction by fraction to the drain. Finally it disappeared into the sewer below.

That night, a man passed by the empty house. He was a baker on his way to begin work. His eyes were half shut with sleep.

He yawned in a slow, deliberate manner and glanced up at the house out of habit.

His feet on the steps made a slapping sound, though he tried to walk quietly. He did not know the house was empty and was careful not to wake the sleeping folk he imagined were inside. But despite his care, still the sound arose. Slip-slap, as he stepped down. Slip-slap and away into the night.

A Guid New Year T 'Ane An Aa

Dawn broke on Glimmerwick long after Lowrie a'Wurlie had risen. These short winter days the sun barely braved the horizon at nine o'clock, and Lowrie's routine demanded a far earlier start than that. He listened to the wireless while stoking the Rayburn stove. Mimie, his wife, was still in the warmth of their bed. Lowrie made tea in readiness for her rising and paced the floor waiting on daylight to clear a path for him, warming his hands in the glow from the opened stove door when he passed.

He stepped outside to let Nell, his Shetland collie bitch, out of her shed. He fed her breakfast on the but end floor. Mimie appeared in the doorway of the room, stretching and yawning.

It was Hogmanay, 1982. It seemed to Lowrie that years went by more quickly than the days had done when he was a boy. Time neither waited for him to do all he wanted, nor allowed him to straddle it and ride its rapid pace as he had once done, off to the whaling in South Georgia, or wherever there was work to be found. Time flickered past him at a rate of knots.

Mimie sat down in the basket chair at the stove's side. Lowrie poured a cup of tea for her and went to the window to gaze out. The wireless was listing the morning news again.

"It's brightnin," he observed. "Come Nell, we'll ging an let da lambs oot."

The dog leapt up and trotted after him. Mimie glanced up and called after him.

"Du'll come in for gruel?"

Lowrie heard her, but didn't bother to reply. As he left the house, he tapped the barometer in the front porch, and watched as the needle dropped so low that it hardly touched on the scale at all.

Outside the air was so empty that breathing seemed an effort. He stopped and took a heavy inhalation of the chilly morning, then walked down along the stone dyke which surrounded the back yard where they grew vegetables, down towards the shore below. He came to the low-roofed, stone-built shed where he kept the home flock of sheep shut in during the winter. He opened the bolt on the rickety door and the familiar smell of his animals met his nostrils full on. Nell waited a little way off, as 1982's lambs pushed past the crofter in a rush, out into the daylight. The flock spread out and began nuzzling at the short grass which had withered and yellow-ochred in the winter's harshness. Lowrie fed them some hay and watched as they ate, feeling proud of their healthy state despite the cold and the rain.

After a while, he called to the dog and turned to walk further down the slope, till he came to the small beach below, where the sea lapped the russet sand with a slow, melodious tongue.

Lowrie listened to the stillness. The world was so quiet that it could only forebode a drastic change. And he was well acquainted with changes. He'd lived through many, through the war, through the fifties when gloom and despondency had abounded in Shetland. The future of the islands seemed bleak then. Many drifted away, disillusioned, to the mainland or the colonies. Even when the sixties brought relative prosperity, Lowrie could not forget what had gone before. He took the changes in his stride.

And when the first whispered promises of oily wealth began in the early seventies, Lowrie a'Wurlie was sceptical. He watched from the house of Wurlie in Glimmerwick while others exchanged their traditional tools for the prospector's pan, and headed for the impending goldmine at Sullom Voe. He warned it would be short lived. He warned them not to place too much faith in the promises of the multinational oil companies. But no one listened to him. To them, he was just an old man whose time had passed him by.

Whatever, Lowrie a'Wurlie was glad he'd stuck to the crofting. He built up a good flock of ewes. He and Mimie lived frugally off the land. She knitted fine hand-lace for one of the shops in Lerwick and sold Fair Isle sweaters to another. They had plenty of fresh vegetables from the back yard and were never short of a leg or two of quality mutton for the freezer. Lowrie was quite content with the way things had worked out. He had lived his life in a place he loved, at his own pace, with no foreman to bawl at him.

Even Mimie's eccentric orbit round about him recently had not swayed his course.

Progress? They could keep it. There was nothing wrong with the old ways. The only changes he was interested in were seasonal ones.

It was a cycle without end; voar, summer, hairst and winter, on and on, life and birth, death and rebirth. Every year, the migratory birds returned and the wild flowers bloomed again. The fish jumped in the voe, and the heather lit the hills.

Lowrie remembered his youth. Was it dotage made the summers seem hotter then? He had run barefoot through the warm fleshy grass, chased by his boyhood companions. He had tumbled without fear of falling into grassy hollows and peaty streams. Barefoot, he had run along the beach at the head of the voe, intent on some important mission — catching spoots or angling sillicks from the rocks; or out in the boat with his father and the other men of Glimmerwick, out beyond the shelter of the land on summer nights that glowed like beacons in his minding. He could picture the lines reappearing over the side of the boat, with hooks bearing fish — desperate sprickling piltocks, furious in the knowledge that their own greed had led them to the taking of the bait. And then home to the fireside, to the tales his father told, of prowess at the haaf fishing or the whaling; tales of heroism tinged with disaster, tales of trowie visitations from under the hill of Glimmerwick, where the goblins lived.

What stories the old folk told the bairns then! Whereas now, the children's entertainment came from that bloody television, that box in the corner of the ben room, talking and singing all day long with utter inanity, of worlds which had no bearing on theirs.

When the first scratchy pictures forced their patterns through the windy island atmosphere, to reassemble on the early black and white sets then gracing a few island homes, no one knew what this new connection with the mainland would bring. Some said that it couldn't be much more influential than the old familiar wireless; surely television wouldn't alter things too much. But Lowrie

a'Wurlie eyed this newcomer with suspicion. He was sharp enough to realise the basic difference between the radio link and the visual one.

Pictures had to be looked at. With the wireless, a body could move around and do things, while listening quite attentively. Imagination created its own pictures.

But with television, things were different. You had to sit there, stationary, like a bairn in a classroom. There was nothing left to the imagination, save to colour in the shapes.

"Dere's no thought required fae a sponge," he would say, quaintly, to anyone who'd listen.

By chance, the signals sent out from the transmitter on top of da Ward o' Bressay, the high conical hill of peat which overlooked the southern entry to Lerwick harbour, reached Glimmerwick in the north of Shetland unobstructed. Albert Henry, Lowrie's neighbour, took an Ordnance Survey map, and plotted the course of the signal. To his amazement, he found that there was every chance that Glimmerwick would receive a picture, despite the thirty-odd miles between the relay station and the settlement. Each potential obstruction seemed to open up conveniently to allow the magic beam through.

So it was that the folk of Glimmerwick (except Lowrie) crowded into Clemmie and Albert's ben room, in time to watch the first trial transmission — the Grand National Steeplechase of 1963.

Albert Henry proudly unveiled his new acquisition, which he had placed in the most prominent position in the room, at the side of the open fire. Mimie a'Wurlie, who had absorbed some of her husband's dubiety, spoke up.

"Yon's a godless ugly box du's bought, Albert."

Everyone was silent as the screen began to flicker. Formless dots took on some kind of shape. Outside the window, Albert Henry stood pointing the heavy ugly aerial in the general direction of Bressay.

"Look," cried Linda, Clemmie's niece, "it's a horse, Clemmie. I can see it!"

She stretched out a girlish finger, which drew the outline of the animal for all to see. People craned their necks towards the equine vision. Mimie, who was clicking away with her knitting needles, looked puzzled.

"Queer looking beast," she muttered, frowning.

Clemmie stared at the screen. She was barely more than a girl herself then, and her eyes were as excited as Linda's. Then, as she identified the shape of the horse, running, her face lit up.

"Oh yes, Linda, I can see it right enough!"

Suddenly the dots of form degenerated to their original snowstorm.

"Albert!" Clemmie shouted. "Albert, it's gone!"

The excitement waned. Linda sighed.

Outside, the bearded sailor cursed under his breath. He moved the large aerial in a slow half circle, trying to relocate the signal. The screen inside flickered again. The shape of the horse re-appeared, only this time it was quite clear, and there, running next to it, was another! Two horses, side by side, racing down the hallowed turf of Aintree, here in this northern living room! It was a miracle!

Everyone shouted at once, even Mimie. Albert stopped dead like a hunting dog, holding the aerial steady. He tapped the ground with his toe.

"I'll sink a post here," he muttered, grinning. "Moor it good and proper."

And so he did. From that day on, television became a part of life in Glimmerwick — and in Shetland as a whole. It was the new thing. Albert and Clemmie showed off their set to whoever cared to come and look. And most folk did. But not Lowrie a'Wurlie.

He was convinced that television would spell the end of the old social custom of 'gyaain aboot da night', the ritual entertaining of one family by another which had been the most popular winter pastime prior to the erection of the transmitter. Lowrie refused to watch on grounds of his faith in tradition. But it wasn't long before Mimie took a liking to the serials she saw at Clemmie's and finally she persuaded him. She had to pay for it out of her knitting money, though. The box arrived, was unpacked, and television made its permanent home in the but-end at Wurlie.

Lowrie still hated it, twenty years on. Even though there were many nights when he sat in front of it, neither thinking of its pictures or its words, yet somehow strangely calmed by its influence. But when a brief and fleeting remembrance of the old times came upon him, of the music people had made then, of the games they played and stories they told, he would smile sadly, knowing that those winter nights of fun were in the past and bound to remain there. Television arrived, and to the seafaring folk of the islands, the huge spindly transmitter pointing like a finger to the heavens became 'da mast', a landmark soon integrated into the eastern horizon, taken for granted like the service it provided.

This had happened in 1963. And here he stood on the edge of 1983. Twenty years had flashed past like a deck of cards in a whist player's hands.

Lowrie spat a fragment of tobacco from his lip, took a last draw on his cigarette, then flicked it into the gently breaking sea. Out across the water, on the other side of the voe of Glimmerwick, the heathery hills rolled grey-brown to the shore. In a sheltered cove where the burn of Setterstoon cut through the peat to enter the sea, he could make out the shapes of some seals lying in the shallows. The stillness spoke with its own tongue. Lowrie listened and watched. Once, all this had been fresh and new. Every day had brought a simple pleasure with it, a reassertion of a rhythm he knew and understood entirely. But since the oil came, age had caught up with him. Since Mimie's rebellion, the house was not the same. It was only in moments like these that he felt the wonder as he had once done continuously.

With a grin which turned into a grimace, Lowrie a'Wurlie turned and walked back up the hill towards the house. His gruel would be ready.

That evening, he raised his glass to 1983. The whisky eased his pain. Ahead lay da voar, spring, with all its toils for the crofter, but Lowrie was tired of the long winter nights and relished the thought of it.

"Happy New Year," he cried, and his cheeks flushed red as he drank back the toast with a nod of his head and a lift of his arm.

Mimie still had her original glass of sherry on the table in front of her. Multi-coloured decorations fluttered in the warm air rising from the stove. Her display of seasonal greetings from the corners of the Commonwealth and less exotic places winked at her and she winked back, sleepy-eyed.

"Wan o'clock an nae first fit," Lowrie muttered, surveying the clock. Mimie yawned, cosy in her seat at the stove's side.

"Wha cares?"

The tick of the clock sounded hollow in their ears. They were waiting on the annual good wishes sent them by telephone, by their two sons in Canada.

Mimie raised herself in her seat. She stretched two short, muscular arms above her.

"I wish da boys wid phone," she said, exhaling the remainder of her yawn, "I could go to bed dan."

Lowrie looked at her with a drunken cunning which made his face seem squint.

"Du's getting awful old, Mimie. Here we are at da start o anidder year an all du can think o is bed," he poked.

"New Year!" she scorned, "I reckon I'm seen enough o dem noo to ken it's just anidder day in da morn."

A silence fell about them then. It was a comfortable room, the but-end at Wurlie, ideally suited to dozing, and well fitted for the kind of routine which the old couple lived. At first glance it might have seemed that the furniture was ill matched, and chosen with no overall design in mind, which was true, but the room had grown old with them and so suited their idiosyncrasies perfectly. The only intrusion on their sleepiness was the sound of the Butlers' entertaining in the Haa house across the turning place.

"All dis incomers, parties and guid kens whit, I never ken whit'll come o it," the crofter muttered, not unkindly, more poking at Mimie's sense of fairness. When bored, Lowrie knew he could raise a little life in the house by pursuing such a tack. But tonight Mimie wasn't listening. Her attentions were split between the television flickering in the corner of the room with its sound turned down and her anticipatory impatience, directed at the telephone.

In truth, Lowrie had nothing against the Butlers. They kept themselves to themselves. With both of them working at the oil terminal, he saw little enough of them. And he would not forget the time in the mid-fifties when he and Mimie had been the only people living in Glimmerwick, after John and Ellen Anderson emigrated to Australia. There had been a time too when the Wurlie folk were on the point of following them. Mimie was very keen. But when it came down to it, they had to think of the boys. They were at school and there was a need to give them security. And even when they went off to the school in Lerwick and the University in Aberdeen, there was still a need to remain; they so loved their holidays at Glimmerwick. So it was lightsome to have neighbours now, wherever they came from, incomers or not. Even if there was little intercourse between the households, it was lightsome to know that they were there.

But as the sound of the party echoed across the turning place, it seemed in some way to exaggerate the loneliness of the Wurlie folk. The fact that a few yards away, strangers were having fun with strangers while the people that belonged here in Glimmerwick were on the other side of the Atlantic.

"Du should go and see if Clemmie's light is still on," Mimie suggested. "Maybe she'll come an first fit de."

"Clemmie? Na na, she'll be lang in bed lass," he answered, and reached out a hand to refill his glass. Mimie's face warned without speech that he had had enough, but the glass was already full and moving to his lips.

And so they waited, alone with their black bun and their shortbread, for the ringing of their telephone, for the same crackly greeting, singing down the wires, like magic all those miles across the ocean; still tied to the bairns after all those years.

Every year, the same words:

"Yes Mam. We're all fine, da bairns too. We miss you."

Mimie cried every year at the sound of her grandchildren's little, Canadian voices. She tried not to, but couldn't help herself. But this year, things were different. She would go there soon. She had the money now. She would see them in their world, at least once.

•••

26

In the bungalow next to Wurlie, Clemmie Henry was watching a staged Hogmanay party on television with all the house lights turned out. Her two children were in bed. She had a glass of vodka in her hand, sweetened with lemonade; a rare occurrence. She smiled glassily at the old jokes. She was thinking of her anniversary — this year would mark twenty years of life in Glimmerwick. Twenty years since she'd married Albert, sixteen years old and full of dreams and girlish notions about how things would be just right. And twenty years too since Linda had come into her life.

Her husband was a merchant seaman, more often away than at home, and though his pay appeared in their bank account monthly, more than enough to see to her needs, things were not the way she had wanted them.

On screen, tartan-clad tele-stars linked arms for the final rendition of 'Auld Lang Syne'. Smooth big band strings and brass sucked the song of its heart, and buried the original sentiment in a mass of plastic nostalgia. Clemmie sang aloud.

"Should auld acquaintance be forgot . . ."

Tears formed in her eyes. The titles appeared on screen, floating upwards. She listened as the national anthem played, then stood up and switched the set off at the mains. She swayed a little, unused to the effects of the alcohol, then groped her way out of the moonlit lounge into the hall. She heard the sound of the Butlers' party, saw the lights through the hall window and thought she might just pop in to wish them well.

Then the voice of her daughter murmured from the bedroom to her left.

"Mam, is it New Year yet?"

Clemmie opened the door a little, enough to poke her head into the room. She saw the shape of Ellen curled up under her bedclothes.

"Yes dear, it's 1983," she answered in a whisper. "Now go to sleep."

Clemmie closed the door quietly and glanced again at the shadows dancing on the curtains of the Haa house. She hesitated, then walked slowly down the hall to her own room, which she

27

entered, switching on a bedside lamp. She began to undress, hanging every item up in her wardrobe as she took it off. She had dressed up for the New Year, out of habit more than belief that she would see anyone. She thought again of Linda, wondered what she would be doing at that moment. Clemmie was thinking that Linda could not have received the message she had left at the workcamp. If she had, she surely would have come. Or would she?

Clemmie faced her mirror, wearing only her petticoat. She released her hair from the bun she had pinned it up in earlier. It fell about her shoulders limply. She picked up a brush and pulled it through the now freed tresses, feeling the teeth of the brush bite into her scalp. She brushed it thirty-six times, one for every year of her life. Thirty-six! She peered at the streaks of grey glinting in the lamp light. She plucked one of the hairs out and broke it into two pieces, surprised at how little resistance it gave. But she knew that the strength of it lay in its persistence; for every one she plucked out, two would grow back. Perhaps she should have done as Linda suggested, perhaps she should have dyed it — but she knew what Albert's reaction to that would have been.

At thirty-six she felt halfway down the tunnel of her life. The light which had illuminated her progress to that point, the light of her youth, had been extinguished by time. Now she was halfway, wishing to retrace her steps but aware that it was impossible. So Clemmie had retreated into her memories in order to ignore the facts of grey hair, shapeless body, lethargic days, lonely nights.

Albert wrote regularly when at sea. But there was a lack of feeling in his letters — too many things left unsaid. She could tell how happy he was on board ship — a different man to the one who moped about the croft, drinking too much and doing too little.

Once he sent her a photograph. Just a small snapshot of him and his first mate, in short-sleeved shirts and neatly pressed trousers. His skin was brown and his beard trimmed. And he was smiling — really smiling! He looked so different from the man she knew that she began to cry. This wasn't the man she knew — but it was the one she wanted.

Clemmie thought of it in gardening terms. Lives bud and grow, just like plants, and two lives planted together, man and wife, should intertwine, not to suffocate but to strengthen. Albert had grown away from her, till the part of him she knew was hardly worth knowing. And without him she drooped, like a climbing plant deprived of its trellis.

She replaced the brush on her dressing table and unrolled the covers of her bed. She switched out the lamp and lay listening to the sound of the party. Music was playing, she could hear laughter and conversation. Her loneliness became all the more pointed. If only Linda had come.

And slowly, the sound drifted further from her. Her power of conscious thought dissembled into dreams, soothed by the vague drunkenness. She closed her eyes and dreamed of a world full of hands, clapping and applauding, but never touching, in which she was a handshake.

•••

In the Haa house of Glimmerwick, a large crowd had assembled, by invitation, to greet the new year, which had arrived as expected, bearing gifts and promising much.

Oliver and Joan Butler had moved to Glimmerwick two years earlier, leaving behind the company house which was their home when Oliver was first transferred north to work on the building of the oil terminal at Sullom Voe. Life on an estate was not to their liking, even if that estate was owned by the company. So they looked around for a suitable property to invest in and settled on the old laird's house at Glimmerwick which was lying in a half completed state following the disappearance of an American entrepreneur whose scheme had foundered some time before. They picked it up at a snip. Apparently the owner had attempted to cash in on the boom when it first was rumoured, only to run out of capital.

The Butlers spared no expense on refurbishing the old house. Oliver was convinced he would make a killing on it when the time came to sell. It was only twenty minutes from the terminal by road.

In the spacious lounge that New Year's Day morning, the hi-fi played loud modern jazz as the party-goers danced. Oliver Butler cast his eyes over the proceedings, one hand deep in his tweed trouser pocket, the other clutching a glass of malt. He was a large, portly figure, with a successful career in chemical engineering stretching out behind him into his past in Saudi. His wife Joan was dancing, a petite figure whose motions were measured to create the maximum possible effect of permanent youthfulness. Her hair was coloured with a reddish rinse which seemed to glow in the firelight behind her.

Oliver sipped his drink and looked about him with pleasure. There seemed to be a warmth radiating from the assembled company which was more than social politeness. This home he had created felt right, somehow, in a way that no other had in the past. He liked the idea of playing the laird.

Almost all the guests were company people like the Butlers, who had followed the exploration rigs north, when oil was discovered which was commercially viable for exploitation. Sullom Voe was an enormous project, the largest of its kind in Europe, constructed out of a barren hillside in a remote part of these cold northern islands. It was an opportunity not only to further individual careers, but also to be involved in something historic.

He could recall quite clearly the first time he saw the site at Graven, back in '76 when the earth-moving equipment had only begun stripping the peat layer from the land in preparation for industrialisation. There had only been a few portacabins stuck in the midst of a sea of mud. The task in hand seemed quite daunting. But as the years slipped by, the metal maze grew and slowly filled to match its blueprint. The thousands of men who had been housed in the workcamps nearby were gone. The boom was over, the monument to technology complete. Huge tankers lay alongside the jetties, filling their tanks with the dead crude from the North Sea wells, like huge insects sucking black nectar to feed the growing young, the research of a twenty-first-century technology. Vast pipes sprawled and intertwined, linking metal vessels and towers, everything working without a break as the workforce came and went, one shift replacing the other. Yes, the boom was over. The terminal would go on producing the vital green-black gold, but the boom was over. And Oliver felt a little sad at its passing.

He could picture the face of the old crofter who had told him of the time when the land which was now Sullom Voe was settled, and how the drift of emigrants had wasted what was then Calback, as it had many other outlying townships. He had spoken too of the Second World War, when Sullom Voe became a base for the armed forces. Oliver saw a strange irony in the fact that this place which had already lived and died twice should once again become so vital, and in the knowledge that its rejection by the indigenous population should lead to today's activity, when the reason for their leaving was precisely because of a lack of opportunity.

Joan Butler tripped across to her husband's side. She was a little tipsy.

"Oliver," she cried, "you look so miserable. Circulate, laugh!"

She slapped him quite hard on his solid shoulder, and returned to the centre of the party. One of the guests approached him. Oliver spoke.

"Enjoying yourself, Bill?"

The young engineer smiled uncomfortably in the presence of a superior.

"Yes thanks, great," he answered.

"Anything interesting happening with you at the minute?"

"No, nothing really. Now that the plant's commissioned, I probably won't be here much longer. In fact I've applied for a job in Aberdeen. Offshore . . ."

"Really?" Oliver took a sip from his glass. "Everyone's leaving," he observed, "I expect we'll be going soon ourselves."

The young engineer looked at him in some surprise.

"You? But you seem so settled here."

"Well we are, but when the work's done, there's not much left but repetition. But I'll miss Glimmerwick, I must admit — or rather I'll miss the house. Joan won't mind so much, she hates the wind so."

They stood for a few silent moments watching the firelight flicker in the hearth and the swaying of the dancers.

"You know it's rather like an end-of-term party," Oliver said thoughtfully, as much to himself as to his companion. And he was right. In one year's time, many of the guests assembled there to greet 1983 would be far away, gone to find another boom, or tucked into the bosom of the company in London or Aberdeen. The workcamps were empty now. The catering staff had been paid off just before Christmas, and only the empty shells of the portacabin complex remained, awaiting their demolition. The peat earth would be cast over them again, the heather would grow back and the echoes of their brief and vigorous past would lie buried in native soil.

The music came to an abrupt end. Joan Butler held up a thin, tanned arm for silence.

"A toast," she cried out, grinning a red lipsticked crescent. "Oliver will now propose a toast."

The eyes of the company turned to their host. He stepped forward to the middle of the floor and raised his glass, exhorting others to do likewise.

"To Sullom Voe," he said, in an easy baritone." May it continue on into many more New Years, operating smoothly and efficiently, as we designed."

It was perhaps a strange toast, more suited to a business meeting, but with a common understanding of its significance, they put their glasses to their lips and drank as one, murmuring 'Hear, hear'. They knew collectively that another twelve months would find them scattered as seeds to the wind, the time which they had shared and the work which they had done growing dim within their memories, decaying into thoughtdust.

•••

Outside, the moon feinted slyly past stiff billowed clouds in a winter sky. The whole of the water of Glimmerwick glistened in the lunar brilliance. The sounds of the party faded into the mirk. Firelight shadows ceased dancing. Final good wishes were exchanged. Car doors slammed shut. Glimmerwick was quiet.

The Butlers' Haa stood stark and tall at the edge of the horse-shoe, once a potent reminder of the power of the laird over the peasant, now the playground of the *nouveau riche* of Shetland — the oil rich.

And alongside the Haa, crouched down into the impenetrable shadows, was the old crofthouse which Lowrie a'Wurlie used as a barn, a symbol of the generations who had left, searching for something which their home could never give them: prosperity.

But the full moon was on the wane. Soon a pale new moon would rise over Glimmerwick, over Shetland, over the world.

•••

Many miles away, on the eastern side of the island, Linda was sitting in a small caravan, deep in the winter dark. She blew out the wavering flame of the candle which had burned till it was wax without taper, and lit another. She was thinking of the folk at home and all that had pushed between her and them, of Sullom Voe and school, of her mother and of Clemmie who had sent her the message to come; but most of all, of the time when it was all fresh and new and the wind blew change from the sea to the east.

PART TWO: 1973-1983

PASSWORDS TO THE NEW PROSPERITY

In 1973, if the eye was closely focused on the horizon round the island, the pencilled-in shape of a distant drilling rig could be seen quite clearly.

In the voar number of the *New Shetlander*, local cartoonist F. S. Walterson depicted the traditional 'auld croftin wife' at the side of her peat stack, setting off a maroon, while at sea the shape of a tanker courting an oil well completed the composition. The sketch was captioned 'Calling him in fae da rig'; a pun centred on the dialect word for 'field' which now had another meaning — that giant wading bird, boring and sucking with its beak beneath the ocean, a modern day sea monster ducking and hiding, out of slingshot on the edge of the visible ocean.

Fears? Suspicions? Uncertainty? Without a doubt! But they were valid fears, coherently expressed, not primitive resistance to technological advance. They were suspicions which had solid foundations.

Native culture and tradition would be swallowed up and disgorged in the rush for money. High-paced, multinational big business would take all and give nothing.

Valid fears, suspicion on good grounds.

Somewhere, a place far from Glimmerwick, men in suits pored over maps and made decisions which would alter the lives of all Shetlanders forever; decisions cold and businesslike, grouped together under the banner-head of exploitation. Claims were being staked: 'This land you do not use here, we will take it, pay you well, make it profitable, for Shetland, for the nation (and for ourselves!).'

Fear, suspicion and uncertainty — passwords to the new age, the keys to the kingdom of Prosperity.

The chosen site for this new industrial panacea was Calbackness, a headland sticking out into, and sealing off, the deep water of Sullom Voe from North Atlantic wrath. Although the out-of-date O.S. maps still showed the little rectangles of habitation, Calbackness was deserted. The nearest community was Graven, a scattering of houses within a mile of the planned oil terminal. But Graven had already been usurped by greater powers, during wartime when it had been a forces base. What remained of this era was an eyesore — disused huts fallen into decay, air raid shelters broken down like bomb site ruins. Even those most strongly opposed to oil had to admit that the multinationals could hardly have picked a less scenic spot to spoil.

But the plans were such that it was not only those places in close proximity which felt threatened. Even in Glimmerwick, twenty minutes from Sullom Voe by road, isolated in its end-of-the-road haven, people were worrying how their lives might be affected.

•••

"Damn dis wadder."

Lowrie was peeking out of the small but-end window at the lashing rain, watching as the ground outside became soggy and puddled. Mimie shivered in her seat at the stove's side.

"Dis cold goes right through me. I canna seem to get a heat in me body ava," she complained, and stretched out her knitting in front of her to see how the Fair Isle pattern was progressing.

"What does du think, Lowrie? Should I use da dark pink or da light?"

"Dark," he replied, without even so much as a glance.

"Dark it is dan," she breathed and reached into the basket at her side where she kept her neatly rounded balls of coloured yarns. She picked up the dark pink and resumed knitting.

Lowrie watched the sea. Out beyond the Eshaness cliffs, the Atlantic churned fiercely, throwing up gigantic waves which warned the knowledgeable away. The small inshore fishing boat which harboured in Glimmerwick had not left its moorings in a week. Wild gales and rain continued to sweep the islands from the north west. Time dragged. It was a weary time for all.

Lowrie had occupied himself by digesting the recently

announced plans for the Sullom Voe developments. He was full of it.

"Brae wi a population o a thoosand," he would say to anyone who would listen. "Man, it'll be a toon!"

He had nightmares filled with streetlamps and supermarkets — in the same peerie place as he had done his courting!

Mimie would smile cryptically at his exaggerated horror. She and Lowrie often took the chance to stir the other up a bit. She took full opportunity by suggesting now and then that she might find a job there, on the catering side.

"It would be a welcome change fae dis weary makkin," she would moan. "My eyes are dat fu o Fair Isle yokes I reckon I'll keel o'er."

Lowrie didn't quite know how to take this. She had a look in her eye which he did not recognise fully, despite their long years together.

Mimie stretched her knitting out in front of her again.

"Na na, Lowrie, surely no dis dark pink," she said, her face aghast, and started pulling out the rows she had just knitted.

"Du has no sense o colour ava, man," she tutted.

Lowrie turned away from the window. He picked up the *Shetland Times* from the floor at his feet and read the sketched plans for the master changes once again. He sighed long and hard with a breathy wheeze come from years of smoking roll-ups.

"Tinks du Mimie, will it ever be da same again?" he murmured, in a tone of voice she barely heard him use. She glanced up at him over the rim of the spectacles she used for makkin. He was getting old, she thought.

"I ken nothin aboot it, Lowrie. Du's spoken aboot nothin else dis lang weary week and I still ken nothin aboot it. It'll tak its course, like athing else."

She stretched out her makkin once again and surveyed it with a shrewd eye.

"Na na," she shook her head, "I don't think dis light pink is right edder."

"Tinks du it will ever be da same again?"

The crofter's question whistled round his head, demanding an answer. But only time could provide that. In his heart, he knew that nothing ever can be the same, that time only goes one way, that what is built cannot be demolished without leaving rubble and a memory of what it was.

The oil boom, then intimated, would mark the land and its people with its brand. His question was not so much 'would things change?' as 'what would be left when the changes were done?'.

And the same question whistled in the winds for the whole of that long weary year; the sounds of its syllables were formed by thousands of worried lips throughout the islands. The pregnancy was painful and weighty, the threatened delivery ominous.

•••

There were some folk of course who were so buried in their own lives as to be oblivious to the offshore threat. Clemmie, Albert and Linda were among these.

In 1973, Albert was home on leave from mid-May until early September and in that time he finally finished building the new bungalow which he had begun four years before. He had done most of the work himself, with the exception of the skilled tasks he felt he wasn't qualified to attempt, like the wiring and the plumbing. And Linda finished her education at the local Junior High in June and was due to go to Lerwick to the High School after the summer. There she would have to stay in the hostel provided for pupils from outlying areas and would only be home in Glimmerwick at the weekends.

It was a year of change for them all. There seemed to be so much happening in their personal lives that the coming of the oil era went almost unnoticed. Deep down among the matters of import which had bearing on their lives, they were no doubt aware of the plans. But in their daily thoughts they had no room for realisation.

The new bungalow was a comfortable dwelling; a far more efficient machine for living in than the crofthouse which had been their home for the previous decade. Great excitement mounted as the day approached when they would transfer their lives the twenty yards from the past into the future. The new house, with its fitted kitchen and tiled bathroom, was the reward from many years of patient hard work — six years raising the money to begin and four to complete the building.

That summer, Albert, Clemmie and Linda lived in a state of transition. The life which had become routine and homely was to be changed, but it was a pleasant removal which they anticipated happily.

A bond had grown between Clemmie and her niece. With Albert away at sea so much, they were alone a lot and they became good friends. There wasn't much difference in their ages really, only twelve years. Linda was four when she came north to Glimmerwick and her memories of a life separate from Clemmie's were few. Only vague recollections haunted her — perhaps she had repressed those early images. And who could blame her if she had? To lose both parents, so suddenly, and she so young. Why, if she could forget, then it was a blessing.

Soon after the girl's arrival, Clemmie received a letter from the mental hospital on the mainland where they had taken her sister. Clemmie read its contents and threw it away, into the red glow of the peat fire in the stove. If the child could forget, then all the better. Clemmie ceased to speak of her sister's return. There would be no recovery. The topic was not touched on at all. Whether Linda forgot, Clemmie did not know, but she was content to let the memory dull. Albert felt differently, though he consented to follow the example of his wife. In his opinion, it was important for the girl to retain knowledge of her belonging. But generally he was silent and did as Clemmie wanted.

Their years in the old house together were contented. They were a family. Linda's youth kept Clemmie young. They laughed a lot, watched television, tended to the garden. Clemmie helped her with her schoolwork and when Albert was home they went for day trips in the car.

Perhaps they spoiled Linda a bit. But as the years went by, they remained childless and it appeared ever more likely she would be the only family they would have. For the most part, she was a cheery child and a pleasure to have about the place. She had a particular aptitude for drawing and painting. Her teacher at the local school encouraged her to think about 'art as a career',

On Parents' Night, he said as much to Clemmie and Albert. While the seaman received this with a grunt, unsure of whether this was a suitable direction for a girl to take, Clemmie smiled and nodded. She liked the thought of Linda as an artist, or even an art teacher. Differ in their notions of her future they might, but there was one thing they did agree on — she was growing fast. After the summer holidays, she would off to the big school in Lerwick. If Clemmie had not had so much to think about with the new house, she would have taken Linda's depaprture badly. But as long as Albert was at home and Linda's leaving not yet imminent, she busied herself setting the new house to rights, trying to get rid of the smell of plaster and paint which hung in the air, gradually moving her treasured possessions across the turning place to the bungalow.

All the talk of oil and Sullom Voe was peripheral. The summer seemed long and warm. Heavy mists lay motionless on the hill of Glimmerwick. The days were humid and soporific. When the heather bloomed it seemed sickly sweet like honey. The folk of the township moved through these mists, going about their work. The summer of 1973; Linda's last real summer at home.

She was thirteen then, no longer a child. Her slim figure was swelling and bulging. Inside her, a sexuality once dormant was awakening. Strange new feelings stirred which suddenly made her interested in her body; how it looked, how it felt. There seemed to be another person inside her, someone who had always been there, but who had been content until this time to hide out of sight of everyone, even Linda herself. But now this other person wanted her body for its own and was preparing to push the child out; like an invader at times although she knew that this was nothing external, like a lord at others, claiming what was its right. As she watched the slow, strange changes in her physical shape, so her mind began to change too, until it was hard to distinguish between cause and effect.

Sometimes the new Linda would fill her totally and she would feel that it was her mind which was forcing these changes on her body. Sometimes the child would resume control and it was her body which felt alien and possessed.

She began to dream heavily, sleeping hours longer than she had ever done before. And in those long hours her mind built worlds which she travelled through alone, often lost, innocent and tempted. The man in the lane recurred in these dreams, but not as the spectre he had been. Now he was a solid man, with a scent and a heartbeat, walking through the night. A man who knew secrets, who knew about the changes, who could teach her. This knowledge he possessed was the key which fitted every lock, but a key newly forged, so hot that she could not bear to touch it for fear of burning herself. But the new person inside her, why she fairly cried out to reach and take it.

Linda retreated from the world around her during that summer. She withdrew from the communal life of Glimmerwick, into her mind where the strange dreams occupied her thought entirely, by virtue of their proliferation.

Clemmie noticed this retreat but she thought it had to do with school and the move to Lerwick. She failed to see the other Linda, the woman inside. She failed to see and did not help to draw her out. She treated Linda as she had always done, as a child and a ward, but the friend who had been there before was gone. Clemmie missed the signs cast down to her and lost her grip on their unity. They became strangers; Clemmie in her new bungalow, Linda wrestling with a new self.

•••

The bungalow which had been so long in the building changed the balance of Glimmerwick. Previously, there were four houses around the turning place — to the west, with wonderful views over the sea beyond, was the house of Wurlie, two storeyed and solid, with a small, angular porch protecting the front door. At the other side, were three houses — in the middle stood the imposing structure of the Haa house and to either side of it, built against its high, stone garden walls, was a crofthouse. The more modern of the two had been the home of the Andersons for many generations, until John and Ellen emigrated, when it was bought over by a relative of theirs, Albert Henry. The other house was much older. It had no upstairs and was used as a barn by Lowrie. Only he could remember it occupied, before the second war when old witchy Bessie Bain lived in it. She had put the fear in Lowrie many a time when he was young. After she died in 1938, the house was left empty — it wasn't worth trying to improve it. Lowrie finally bought its lease for a few pounds and stored hay there.

The Haa house lay empty for many years too. At the end of the nineteenth century, a mill owner from Lancashire bought it from a titled family who had run into debt. He didn't realise how far Shetland was from the mainland of Scotland so his country estate weekends were few. When a cousin of his inherited it in the early twenties, she came to live there for a while and ran the house as a small, exclusive hotel, offering prime fishing on the estate. She was a stiff woman with a dour face who hardly spoke a word to the tenants living next door to her. When the war broke out in '39, she left and the Haa stood vacant for many years. But even when empty, the house still exacted a kind of rule over the crofting folk of the area; no stones dared penetrate its windows. As the land of the estate was sold off bit by bit, and the walled gardens fell into a wild state of weeds, the house grew lonely and sad to look upon but still retained its dignity. Glimmerwick was still under the nose of its laird. The Haa house was his aged, decrepit retainer.

Thus when the new bungalow was built alongside the house of Wurlie, the balance of the settlement shifted. Now there were two occupied dwellings across from the Haa, and none on its side. The three houses on the east watched life at a distance — the Haa, stern and forbidding; the two crofthouses, one full of the smells of animals and hay, the other still warm with the scent of people.

•••

It was not unusual for a car to arrive in Glimmerwick, un-announced and alien. On Sundays especially, people would stop their vehicles and look about them for a while before driving off. Sometimes walkers or birdwatchers would park there while they headed north along the coastline. Lowrie might see them and say hello, but then again, he might not.

It struck Mimie as strange, then, the fuss which he made one Sunday that summer when a car stopped outside the Haa house. He watched from the ben-end window, fidgeting.

"Wha is yon, tinks du Mimie?"

Mimie was watching the Sunday matinee on television.

"Na look Mimie, see," he urged her.

"Lowrie, will du sit doon! What's wrong wi de, man?"

"It's dis folk here. I reckon dey're snooping aboot da Haa."

Outside, the car had stopped at the gate of the house and two figures entered the gardens of the laird's abode through the rotten wooden gate, now swinging from its hinges tenuously. It was an old car in immaculate condition, a pre-war model, with its top folded down. On the back seat a large Red Setter sat waiting, panting heavily. Perhaps it was the fact that the strangers had entered the sacred garden which annoyed the crofter. He didn't know or care. Like a collie, the hair at the back of his neck had pricked up at the sight of them. He scuttled through to the but-end to fetch the binoculars he used for watching the passing ships at sea, then hurried back to the front of the house, pushed the lace curtain aside and focused in on the two men. Just as he got them in view, they disappeared behind a wall.

"Damn," he mouthed.

Mimie craned her neck round from her seat on the sofa.

"What's du doing, Lowrie?"

"Nothing, Mimie. Watch dy film," he mumbled, screwing his face up as he searched for the visitors among the walls and dykes in front of the Haa. For a moment Mimie watched him with a faint glimmer of disapproval on her face. Then she turned her attention back to the television, where Ginger Rogers and Fred Astaire were dancing and singing simultaneously, backed by a hidden orchestra. Lowrie waited, his eyes like a hoody crow's. He caught sight of something moving and the binoculars shot up to his face in an instant.

"Aha!" he breathed, twirling the central focusing mechanism.

There, he had them! A man of about thirty-five in a long fur coat, with another, shorter and darker. Lowrie tried to memorise their faces. The taller man had wavy blond hair and wore thin-rimmed spectacles. He was talking to the other as if he was giving orders, as if he was the leader and his companion the subordinate. Lowrie kept up this vigil for fifteen minutes, putting the binoculars aside for a time, then picking them up again. On the television, Fred and Ginger danced.

"Isn't this a Lovely Day to be caught in the rain," they sang, spinning in elegant circles across the screen.

Mimie sighed. "Why don't dey still make films like dis?"

"Eh?"

Mimie turned to look at him.

"Lowrie! Whit is du doing?"

"Ssh, dey're coming back."

"Wha's coming back? Whit's du in such an agitation for?"

Lowrie ducked away from the window. "Have a look oot yon window," he whispered. "See yon twa men?"

Mimie did as he suggested. "I see dem."

"Dey're been snooping aboot da auld Haa."

Her expression became one of scorn. "Du's an auld fool. A couple o folk oot for a drive on a Sunday, an du's acting like du wis James Bond."

"I'm telling de, Mimie, dere's something queer going on. I can feel it in me bones."

At this, she burst into a grin, then laughed loudly while Lowrie frowned.

"I'm telling de," he went on, "du'll see. It's all to do wi dis oil."

With that, he rose up and left the room with the binoculars in his hand. The two strangers got into their car outside and sat for a few minutes talking. Mimie could see their mouths move from the ben-end of Wurlie. Then they drove off and she went back to watching the musical.

But Lowrie was right. During the next fortnight, the veteran car appeared twice more in Glimmerwick. On both occasions, the two men inspected the old house and when they arrived a third time, they brought with them a local builder who carried a clip-board and stood making notes while the strangers talked.

By this time, everyone was interested, even Mimie. The man in the long fur coat and his dark lieutenant was the subject of all the talk of the district. Various stories arose from the hotel in Hillswick, where they were staying. Some said he was an actor, others a male model or a dress designer. Perhaps he was all three. Whatever, he was an alien type, an American, not like the men of the north land at all. He drove fast through the summer-green fields on the spindly, single track roads, blowing his horn at the ruminant sheep lounging on the hot tarmac, disturbing the rural quiet.

Linda spoke to him one day, the first of the Glimmerwick folk to do so. It was at the telephone kiosk at the head of the voe, about half a mile from the township in the middle of nowhere. She was on her way home from a friend's house in nearby Hamnavoe when she came upon him, pacing up and down outside the kiosk, whistling loudly. He was alone. When he saw her approaching, he stopped his tune and stepped forward. She hesitated, then walked towards him — there was no other route home.

"Does this thing work?" he called out to her, when she was still a good way off. She blushed, and shrugged.

"I wanted to call New York," he went on, "but I can't figure out if this thing is out or not."

She was close to him now and her shyness became more pointed.

"Hey I won't bite," he grinned, seeing her state.

"I ken," she stammered, smiling awkwardly. "I . . ."

For a few seconds they stood in the middle of the road facing each other. She seemed to feel a strange warmth emanating from his face. Then he asked again.

"Look, I don't suppose you'll ever have had much call to use this thing, but I was trying to get New York. I've never seen anything like it, it must be an antique. What do these buttons mean, A and B?"

She shrugged again. "I'm sorry, nobody ever uses it muckle. I don't ken."

With that she pushed past him and began running up the hill towards the houses, her face reddening with each step. As she ran she began to berate herself for her foolishness. Why had she gone to pieces in front of him? Everyone in Eshaness and Hillswick was dying to meet him and when the chance presented itself to her, she could only stammer. She began to wonder if this was some part of the changes, if she was losing something more than simply her childhood. Then she saw his face in her mind, as fresh as a photograph, and something inside her ignited.

Linda said nothing of their meeting. It became another secret in a summer ever more furtive.

But soon the stranger's purpose became common knowledge. Whether he had tried to conceal his mission by preserving the air of mystery about him or not, there was nothing more certain than leakage. Curiosity demanded it.

Before long, everyone knew — the old Haa at Glimmerwick was to become a luxurious hotel, catering for the wealthy visitors which Sullom Voe would bring in its wake. Business people, with limitless expense accounts, who required a little more in the way of comfort than the existing hotels could provide. Plans were drawn up and a firm of local builders were contracted. Glimmerwick came alive with a whole fleet of strange cars and vans, flitting in and out the single-track road while people measured up, surveyed and plotted. At the centre of it all, the tall American in the long fur coat stood directing the unfolding story with style and assurance.

The old house was stripped of its interior — floors, lining, stair-cases — everything — ripped out and piled in heaps in the walled gardens. Even those forbidding eyes, the windows, from where the lairds of past eras had watched their serfs and tenants toil.

Lowrie a'Wurlie could only gape. Within one month of the work beginning, Glimmerwick was altered forever. The last vestiges of the laird's power lay splintered in the gardens, impotent and weak, cracked and old. The new owner brought his panting dog, his noisy car and gregarious personality, and with these tools he ripped out the past like a page from a history book. Linda watched it all from hidden places only she knew of. She remembered something she had seen on television, a programme on the supernatural, in which it was suggested that houses record the actions of those who live in them, and store these in some kind of memory, awaiting the psychic mind to set the projector rolling. If this was true, in some mysterious manner, then this stranger was the destroyer of the reels of paranormal film lurking in the depths of the old Haa at Glimmerwick. In tearing off the roof and exposing the stone of the house to the summer sun, he unwittingly exposed the undeveloped film and wiped the darker ages of oppression from the settlement of Glimmerwick.

Yet Lowrie felt an ache in the soul of the place, a space left gaping there which had previously been filled by the aura of the Haa. The speed of the change was startling, and the course ahead seemed so uncertain.

Fear, suspicion and uncertainty: passwords to the new age, the open sesame of oil. For Lowrie and Mimie the threat was real — thirty years of their lives together were about to be guillotined, to be lost on the other side of the oil era, visible yet untouchable.

To Linda, still learning about living, change was not so much a threat as a gift to anticipate.

For Albert and Clemmie, the changes and their effects were ambiguous. They themselves were just beginning a new chapter in the bungalow, but still, they were used to their routines.

Albert Henry was a straightforward sort of man. He said what he thought and lived according to his notions of what was right. While not a churchgoer, there was a particular rigidity within him which was an expression of his Presbyterian upbringing.

He left school at fifteen to join the Merchant Navy, like his father and grandfather before him. He was capable of carrying his education further, but had been a sailor from birth, only truly happy when in a boat. As a boy, he had spent his summer holidays in Glimmerwick with the Andersons, cousins of his mother. The youthful love and the associations with freedom which he felt for the place stayed with him. Years later, when John and Ellen Anderson emigrated, he bought their croft and brought his young wife north to live.

Albert loved the life at sea. If asked to explain exactly why, he could not answer, but he knew he loved it. It was in his blood. Being bright and not afraid of responsibility, he quickly ascended the ladder of seniority, till all that remained for him to achieve was his Master's Ticket and his own command. He would have that too, in time: Captain Albert Henry. He knew that it was well within his reach and did not question this. Pride, to Albert, was not a sin but an essential. To know one's true worth, to behave with dignity, to wear one's pride like a well-tailored coat was only right and natural.

Not that his life did not have its difficulties. He was away at sea so much that he found it hard to readjust to life in Glimmerwick when he returned. He wasn't as close to Clemmie as he wanted to be. But then she had Linda for company. Albert was glad of that. Yet he believed he knew the islands intimately. All over Shetland, there were people he could honestly call 'friend'. He was familiar with every winding road and the community lying at its conclusion; he knew the waters round about, with all their complexity, as well as any inshore fisherman.

What perhaps he did not understand was the process of social change taking place. He was rarely at home for more than a few months at a time and so the sequence of events was lost to him. This lack of understanding which could only be gained by living in the place constantly, sensitive to all the undercurrents about. He was watching a film which had been edited so severely as to lose its continuity — he filled in the spaces with imaginings, or remembered moments out of context. Perhaps in a way he was aware of this. Perhaps he sensed it but refused to acknowledge it. Whatever the reason, when the plans for the Haa at Glimmerwick were announced, Albert's reaction was quite irrational. For the folk who had lived through the intimations of the coming boom, the scheme did not come as too much of a shock. Lowrie had almost predicted it. They, like him, had seen the pattern unfolding.

But Albert's view of the Shetland of 1973 was a blinkered one and the developments took him by surprise. That sense of shock was to stay with him for a long time to come. He could never quite grasp the way of oil. He was always running just behind the pack, barking at the leaders. Every fresh shock stung him just as hard as the first and each time he was stung, he yelped and bit whatever was closest to him.

"Bloody conman," he muttered, reading Clemmie's letter on board ship, telling him of the American's scheme.

"Flashy cars, flashy money, bloody conman."

•••

Throughout the winter, work continued on the Haa house. Extensive renovation was required to the structure of the building, as well as the complete refurbishment of its interior. By Christmas, the old servants' quarters were completed and the American, Stokowski to name, moved in, while the builders continued their labours in the other parts of the house. Stokowski had strange ideas on the design. He had the old, four-storeyed interior ripped out and replaced by three, so that the resultant rooms were still larger than before. He replaced the old slate roof with glass! He imported special timber from America because he felt the local stock was inferior. The builders smiled to themselves as they worked, cracking sly slanders on their employer, more used to reroofing barns and crofthouses. They looked on the American as an idler who was somehow short of the shilling; a man still caught up in the fantasies of boyhood which they themselves had long since given up. But even so, to his face they were servile and polite, as he wandered about the site in his long coat (he wore no other), smoking Turkish cigarettes, all the time bearing a look of intense relish, as if he was enjoying a secret morsel of supreme delicacy, swallowing the titbit then bringing it back into his mouth again, as a cow passes its fodder from stomach to stomach.

Then in February, a very strange thing happened. Unprompted by the local grapevine, a woman from Brae came to keep house for him — but not any woman: this sphinx was a part of the folklore of the north land, having been married three times and enmeshed in a score of other explosive affairs. She wore her past proudly, as battle scars, but in the eyes of the community she was a woman lost. She dyed her hair a startling shade of henna red, wore mini skirts and high heels; her stockings were always bulging with ladders.

51

Stokowski's credibility lurched low. Lowrie found it hard to believe that this jet-setter, as he called him, should have chosen such a woman to housekeep for him. The crofter couldn't stop his tongue from talking.

But to everyone's astonishment, no scandal emerged from the shell of the half renovated house. Whatever relationship the odd couple might have had, no one had any real cause to gossip — though gossip they did. For a number of weeks, the unlikely duo came and went, she cooking and cleaning and he supervising the workforce.

No one but Linda noticed how the housekeeper changed. Her face was so well known that no one bothered to look at it closely. But the grey roots which had always threatened to push the colour from her hair disappeared. Her choice of lipstick colour mellowed also. No one but Linda noticed, but the housekeeper seemed to be drawing something potent and life-giving from her new role. And while Lowrie waited for some overstepping of the mark, a soft aura of contentment settled over the reborn Haa house, sealing it off from malice.

And then Stokowski left on business. He was due to return in a few weeks. The housekeeper stayed on, watching for his car on the brow of the hill, waiting for the telephone to ring. Weeks went by and became months. The workmen realised that no further payment was forthcoming and ceased their labours. Boilersuited men packed their tools into vans and drove away. The housekeeper waited. Her hair began to show silver at the roots. Her stockings burst into ugly ladders. Sadly, she conceded it was time to go; she had never pressed her employer for information on his movements and had no way of contacting him. She could wait no longer.

Once again she found herself with a suitcase in her hand, moving on. The day she closed the door for the last time, Linda was home from school and was watching from behind one of the moss-covered garden walls.

She heard the woman speak to her reflection in the window.

"All men are the same, whether it's whisky or brandy you get just as drunk and just as hungover," she mouthed.

But Linda had seen her change and knew that she was lying to herself. He had given the woman a brief but lingering warmth, had entered her island home and had taken her as he found her, ignoring all the gossip. Linda knew that in this place where tradition rooted people like plants, he had the power of flight, the power to alter habit — a power of no direct force, powerful because it was free. The girl saw this and understood that this was no isolated occurrence but a symbol of what was to come.

The housekeeper left and the Haa lay empty. No noisy cars, no giant dogs — Glimmerwick was returned to its previous tranquillity, but forever marked. The windows in the Haa no longer whispered phrases from the past. Whatever secrets they had concealed were now told. The laird's seat had become an oil age folly.

Despite the abrupt end which the American's disappearance brought to the work at the Haa, there was no easing of the worry which had fixed itself in Lowrie a'Wurlie's mind. He knew that this was merely a setback, that there would be others who would come and fulfil the future Stokowski had promised, if not in Glimmerwick then elsewhere. The planned development was such that Lowrie never once relaxed. He knew the scheme off by heart.

'The oil terminal will provide storage capacity for the crude oil from Brent and Ninian fields — there will be a processing plant which will flash off the hydrocarbon gas from the volatile crude and a fractionation plant to split this gas into its components.'

Lowrie made it his business to know. He visualised the whole thing spreading its influence from Lerwick north to Glimmerwick. New estates of houses would be built for the permanent staff. Workcamps for the thousands of tradesmen involved in the construction. The island road network would have to be brought up to standard. The workcamps would need staff from the local workforce; cleaners and chambermaids, chefs and barmen.

Although the American had left, there would be others. There would be thousands, flooding north, looking for the big money.

Lowrie knew what was happening. Despite his apprehension, he was fully aware. And so was his wife.

53

Mimie Manson was a very intelligent woman, though she liked to hide this under a gloss of jollity. She always had a smile for folk, a droll comment followed by a rosy-cheeked grin. She was rather short and overweight, with a large maternal bust and strong thick legs which jabbed up and down like twin pistons when she walked. She was a woman of habit — her days were set to a steady routine — but she was not so stiff as to be immovable. On the contrary, her routine existed precisely for the purpose of allowing her time to do things she wanted to, by assisting her to finish her chores without ever having to think too deeply about them.

And when they were over, she relaxed while knitting Fair Isle and reading at the same time, as the television chattered in the corner of the room. She had an extensive knowledge of things far beyond the sphere of her own life, gleaned from years of self-education by the stove's side in Wurlie. Had she been born a generation later, no doubt she would have followed the academic path to its conlcusion, at a university. But Mimie's schooling had been cut short by the war, when daughters were needed more than ever around the croft. And in those days there was little chance of further education, unless your parents were well off. Mimie's folk, kind and goodhearted as they were, never had much money to spare. The croft was hard pressed to support the family, let alone a girl at school long after her natural time.

So when she was seventeen and the war was over, she went to work on the mainland of Scotland as a maid in a large country house, near Linlithgow. She didn't care for the life at all, though the people were kind enough to her.

She missed her family, the barren moorlands and the open spaces. The trees made her feel enclosed. She missed the spirit of willingness to help a neighbour she was familiar with, where poverty was a constant adversary, aggravated by a poor summer or a loss at sea. She didn't stay long on the mainland. Her folk agreed to take her back and she found a job in a shop in Brae. She was good with figures and liked the sociable side of the work, meeting all the folk from round about and getting their news.

She worked there until she was twenty, when she married Lowrie Manson of Glimmerwick and went there to live, with him and his old mother. At first her mother-in-law had resented the presence of another woman in the house. But within the year, Mimie was pregnant and all the ill-feeling was forgotten. In the spring, with the lambing under way, she gave birth to twin boys. They named them after their grandfathers, as was the custom.

The years seemed full after that. She channelled all her impressive energies into giving the boys the chances she had been denied. At school they won prizes every year. Before she knew it, they were sitting O-levels and Highers and were off to university in Aberdeen.

When it was all over, when the twenty-three years of academic achievement ended with a three-day excursion to the south, for their graduation, when Mimie sat down and really thought about it, she realised that the education she had so prized had taken her children from her. They were no longer Andrew and Theo Manson of Glimmerwick, they were B.Sc. Hons. of Aberdeen University. They graduated into colour photos on her mantelpiece, where they sat stiffly smiling in their robes and mortar-boards, like well-fed birds of prey gazing down on her.

Canadian stamps covered the top right-hand corners of the envelopes they posted to her now — they both emigrated, within a year of each other, still twins with their fates tied together. She was determined she would go there one day, to see them in their world, with or without Lowrie. It was her prize too, after all.

So Mimie too watched the reports of the Sullom Voe expansion with interest. She listened carefully to the news about the workcamps. She made up her mind and waited. She would find a way to Canada all right. She could work as well as anyone.

•••

Albert Henry and his niece Linda both left Glimmerwick in August. Clemmie suddenly found herself alone in the new house. While she had known all along that this would happen, she hadn't prepared for it. There had been so much to do around the house.

Linda still came home at weekends, of course. But it wasn't the same. The closeness they had shared, already stretched by the changes of the summer, now threatened to snap like a taut elastic band. Linda telephoned during the week from the girls' hostel she stayed in. She had lots to tell, lots of stories about her new acquaintances, the new school, new everything. Clemmie tried her best to be interested, to become involved in her niece's new world, but the names kept slipping from her mind, she had no faces to attach them to. She became muddled and Linda grew annoyed. Despite this, Clemmie was glad for her. She seemed to have suffered no awkward acclimatization, no homesickness. And she seemed to be doing well at her lessons.

In Glimmerwick, winter was approaching all too quickly. Lowrie was at work in the fields below the settlement, cropping the corn and the hay. The brief summer green was already transforming into autumn's beige and gold. Clemmie walked around her new home in a dream, opening all the doors and windows to disperse the smell of paint, staring at the new order of things. The new carpets were fitted and the furniture from the old house arranged, yet Clemmie felt there was a part of her still lingering in the dark little crofthouse across the turning place. She seemed to be tired all the time, she had no appetite. She wanted someone to share this experience with, someone to talk to. But they had gone, both Albert and Linda, and she was by herself.

•••

The High School in Lerwick, although officially comprehensive, still retained its old grammar school identity by means of the catchment area system of Junior Highs dotted around the outlying corners of the islands. This system meant that apart from the pupils who lived in Lerwick itself, the classes had all been weeded out, streaming the brighter pupils like Linda towards academic achievement, whilst most of her former classmates in Brae were left to idle out the months until they were old enough to leave. From Lerwick, the cream would be skimmed off to the mainland of Britain, where they would become free from geographical bias, able to integrate into urban life and the professional class.

Linda was taking tender steps along this pathway. She had

fixed her eye on a place at Art College. At the Junior High in Brae, she had been the art teacher's favourite, and he had given her ideas. Things were different in Lerwick. There were others who shared her talent and her ambition. One of her room-mates, a girl from the island of Unst named Elsie, became one of her rivals. Linda felt inferior to Elsie's more worldly ways and held back from her. Elsie enjoyed teasing Linda. She used the other girls in their room as tools in this game, by pointing Linda out as a figure of fun. Elsie gave her the nickname 'Piltock', because she said her eyes were like those of a fish. The name travelled throughout the hostel and others joined in the teasing.

Linda would lie in bed after lights out, long after the others had ceased poking fun at her, thinking about Glimmerwick and how kind the folk had been to her there. So kind and yet so calm in the way they administered their goodness, so that Linda had never considered it until she was confronted with a less pleasant environment. She dreamt again of the man in the lane, penetrating through her outer skins, piercing her. She was sad and homesick. She began to wish she had stayed at school in Brae, where she was liked by the other children.

But she was blessed with a certain streak of obstinacy which made her dig her heels in. She took the ribbing for a time, and then one day exploded.

The incident took place in the dark. After lights out, as usual, the girls lay and talked for an hour or so before sleep. Elsie generally led the conversation.

On the night when Linda's bubble of silence burst, Elsie began by telling the other girls that Piltock wasn't really a girl at all. She said that if a girl hadn't started her periods by the time that she went into third year like them, then she would grow up to be a lesbian. The other girls in the dormitory giggled. Linda shut her mind off.

Elsie went on.

"And my sister says it runs in families, that mothers can be lesbians too. Was your mother a lesbian, Linda?"

The girls all sniggered at Elsie's language, at the forbidden words she used so casually. But they were laughing more out of a feeling of dread than amusement. Their forced mirth faded away. Suddenly, out of the dark and the quiet, Linda released a scream and leapt across the room to Elsie's bed where she began beating and scratching and pulling at her tormentor's hair. Elsie screamed too, and suddenly the whole room was illuminated with anger. The others started crying out as well, their dread transformed into terror. Some kind of murder was taking place, and they wailed like ancient crones around the cauldron, shaking with fear as the two figures writhed in moonlight from the night outside. Then, as suddenly as Linda's anger had erupted, the door of the dormitory opened and the light went on. The grown-up figure of the house-mistress filled the doorway and her voice screeched at the two girls, who had fallen from the bed and were continuing their teeth-and-fingernail scuffle on the floor.

Linda and Elsie were both 'confined to barracks' for a month. The matron threatened to expel them if they ever stepped out of line again. Linda was terrified that news of her fight might reach Glimmerwick.

Yet the incident was soon forgotten, and when the period of confinement was over, Linda found that she had been accepted. Even the older girls now treated her as a person, and her nickname became a thing of the past. She began to open up to people, and much to her surprise, she actually became friendly with her enemy, the loud-mouthed Elsie. Their friendship firmed. They laughed a lot. Elsie taught Linda how to smoke and swear and how to walk with an imposing swagger. They started hanging around Commercial Street at night with a crowd of boys from the school. It was a lifestyle alien to her, after the tranquillity and Presbyterian reserve of Glimmerwick, and for many months she carried a great sense of guilt around with her, hiding the truth of her new life from Clemmie when she went home at weekends. Yet there was no turning back. She had reached her first real crossroads, had chosen to fork along the sinister direction towards adulthood. To retreat again into the sweet naivety of childhood was impossible.

The stiff chrysalis which had encased her during those last summer months in Glimmerwick was cracking open, and inside one could glimpse the intricate and boldly coloured patterns of her adult wings. The woman lurking inside began to show herself. Elsie provided the catalyst that Clemmie had been unable to offer. The hatching process was under way.

•••

That Christmas, Clemmie had a little cash to spare. With Linda away at school through the week, her housekeeping went further than before. She decided to spend the extra on her niece. It was her's in a sense, after all.

In Lerwick, on Commercial Street, Christmas shopping, Clemmie wandered around with a wad of notes in her red vinyl purse, gazing into shop windows, trying to decide what to buy. The narrow winding street was lit up with coloured lights and seemed to Clemmie to resemble some corner of Santa's grotto.

Clemmie spent a whole day walking up and down the little street. She knew that Linda wouldn't be impressed by a cuddly toy or a doll. She knew that it was all about records and clothes and make-up now, but she didn't know what was fashionable.

Finally she spent the money on a small transistor radio, and carried it happily back to Glimmerwick where she carefully wrapped and hid the gift.

On Christmas morning, Clemmie entered Linda's bedroom with the parcel in one hand and a cup of tea in the other. Linda sat up in bed and pushed tousled hair away from her face. Clemmie smiled at her.

"Linda," she said nervously, holding the present half hidden behind her, "I had a bit of money . . ."

The words drifted away from her. Why was she explaining? It was Christmas after all, the time for giving presents. She simply handed the gift to her niece, placed the cup on the bedside table and waited. Linda unwrapped the radio hurriedly, ripping the paper that Clemmie had chosen so carefully. Her face broke out into a wide grin when she saw the contents.

"It's super, Auntie, really super," she said happily, then lay back on her bed smiling.

A sharp, tight feeling coiled around Clemmie's heart. Why had she said 'Auntie', why not 'Clemmie' as before? Clemmie laughed quietly, and accepted the girl's gratitude, but she knew that she had failed in her objective. She had tried to rekindle their closeness by giving Linda a special gift. But where was this space coming from, this gap which was squeezing itself between them? She sighed and left the room. In the kitchen she placed four eggs in a pan of water and resigned herself to the changes.

Linda lay on her bed, staring into space. Clemmie's kindness had exaggerated the sense of guilt she harboured over her deceitful subterranean life in Lerwick after school. The secret swearing and the smoking and the drinking made her feel tainted and dirty. She looked at the little radio her aunt had given her and felt a tear ooze out from her eye.

•••

In early February of 1974, Clemmie went to the doctor's surgery in Hillswick. She explained that she had been feeling tired and lethargic, and that she was off her food. The doctor listened carefully, nodding at her from behind his desk. When she had said her piece, he breathed a sigh and tapped his pen on the desk top.

"I just . . ." Clemmie hesitated.

"Go on?"

She shook her head. The doctor stood up and looked at the open file in front of him.

"You're Albert Henry's wife? How is he?" he asked her, without looking up. Clemmie was taken by surprise by his familiar tone.

"Fine," she answered. "He's away at sea just now."

"I've sailed against him at the regatta," the doctor explained. "Good sailor, knows his stuff."

Dr Mathieson was a medical man by profession, but had he had his life over again, he would probably have followed Albert to sea. His practise in Shetland hardly offered him the opportunity to advance medical science in any way, but it did afford him a comfortable life and the chance to spend his summers on board his small yacht. He was prone to categorising his patients as fellow sailors and landlubbers.

He sat down again at his desk, and for a while looked out the surgery window to the cove below where he could see his yacht bobbing on the waves. Then he turned his attentions back to Clemmie.

"Is it possible that you might be pregnant?"

Clemmie shook her head in disbelief.

"I . . . I . . . she stammered, "I don't know. Well maybe . . ."

"I'd like to take a test . . ." the doctor said quietly. "From what you've told me, I have a notion Albert may be going to become a father."

The test proved positive. Clemmie was thrilled. She wondered if her body had somehow repressed conception till she had built her nest, some manifestation of instinct.

Certainly, it couldn't have happened at a better time. And now that she knew what it was that ailed her, she came to like the feelings inside her. The knowledge that a whole new creature was growing, a creature endowed with the marvel of life.

This would be no byre birth, no simple grazing animal, but a human being, her own child!

She became calmer and less on edge. She ate more. The knowledge that she was capable of maternity, of continuing the species, seemed to fulfil her. After years of playing the role of mother, she was finally to perform the reality. It felt, to her, like a great honour, and one which she was modestly worthy of. The outside world, beyond the walls of her new and cosy home, drifted far away. There might have been an earthquake or a murder on her doorstep and she wouldn't have cared, so long as she and her swelling womb were untouched.

Albert, at sea on board ship, was stunned. Immediately he arranged leave around the dates of her expected confinement.

"It'll be a boy, I ken it," he boomed down the phone to her from Gibraltar.

"Maybe," Clemmie replied, smiling to herself.

Linda took the news strangely. Clemmie had expected her to react strongly, but instead, the girl said little. Like the gift of the radio, the calm, unaffected way she received the news made plain to her aunt how she had changed.

Not that Clemmie cared now. In fact, she was glad. Although they had shared much when Linda was young, Clemmie wondered if perhaps some sense of responsibility to her might have prevented earlier conception.

Whatever, Linda had chosen. She was the one who'd grown away from Clemmie, not the other way about. Clemmie owed her nothing but a home at weekends and holidays, she'd paid her dues a hundred times over. She'd given Linda everything and more since she'd arrived there. If it was over, then Clemmie was glad; her own life waited, her own family.

At school in Lerwick, Linda's early friendship with Elsie McMaster from Unst had become solid. At the same time, she was developing a relationship with a boy from one of the other islands, Michael, who was in his final year at school and was already accepted for art college in Edinburgh.

It was a casual friendship. She knew that he had other girl-friends. But she didn't mind that too much. He was a door into an older world, a world where the woman she was becoming felt at home.

He had a car. An old banger. And he had friends who had left school, he went to parties where there was alcohol, he smoked and drank.

He was very cool, very self-contained. He hardly spoke to her when they went out together, except to tell her about some book or other he'd been reading or the work of some artist she'd never heard of.

Sometimes she wondered why he should have asked her out in the first place. She was aware that she wasn't particularly pretty, and she knew by his expression when they were together that he felt uncomfortable with her among his older friends.

Elsie thought he was conceited. Sometimes Linda did too. But there was something special about him too, in her eyes. Though she didn't expect their relationship to last beyond his leaving school, she was determined to get as much as she could from him while she could, to try to pin down what it was that he had that attracted her. And if there had to be the odd sacrifice along the way, so be it. The woman in her was hungry.

The night when it finally happened, in the back seat of his car, after they had drunk a bottle of cheap wine and had eaten greasy chips from their newspaper packages, she laughed.

His breath made clouds of moist air in the cold atmosphere of the night. Street lights shone yellow through the steamed-up glass. She held her breath and it was easy. A little painful at first, but easy.

"You're really good," he said afterwards, smoking a cigarette in glassy thought.

She smiled and kissed him.

"Thanks," she said and put her hand on his knee.

"I don't mean that," he said sharply. "I mean at art. I've seen your drawings in the art room."

Linda withdrew her hand, surprised.

"Oh!" she exhaled.

"A screen print, and some drawings. I reckon you've got something."

"What?"

He smiled. "Talent I suppose."

After that evening, Michael ignored her at school. If they passed in the corridor, he would smile vaguely. It seemed to Linda to be a sneer which said . . . "I *know*".

She was disturbed. He seemed to have penetrated her, taking something from her, not her virginity, but something more vital, something which she herself was not truly aware of.

•••

"Lowrie, it'll make no difference whit du says, I'm decided."

Mimie Manson had just broken the news to her husband that she was applying to the workcamp at Firth for work as a chambermaid.

Lowrie said nothing. He simply sat down by the stove and pulled off his working boots. It was one o'clock, dinner time, and a pot of stew bubbled on the hotplate.

After a time, Lowrie spoke.

"Mimie, Mimie, whit is du thinkin o?"

His wife snapped back at him, as if she had anticipated his opposition.

"Canada!" she said, then turned to the stove where she stirred the stewpot.

Lowrie placed his boots on the small stool in front of the stove. He shook his head slowly, without looking up at her.

"Lass lass, we'll win to Canada withoot dis. I'm been saving," he said seriously. "I'll have a cheque for da oo shortly, and in da hairst, der'll be lambs ta sell. Du doesna have to go to dis god-forsaken camp to work."

She spooned the stew onto the waiting plates.

"I'm decided, Lowrie," she said in a resolute tone. "Dis way, I'll be able to save too. Dan next year we'll both be able to go and see da boys, and we'll have money to spare."

Lowrie shook his old grey head again. He had been aware of Mimie's thoughful silence lately, and had known that she was plotting something. But this!

Suddenly the fact that she would be away from home all day hit him.

"I'll never see de," he exclaimed, glancing up at her.

"It'll no be forever," Mimie answered. "Come and get dy dinner."

He took up his seat at the table, began to eat, his eyes firm on his food, not once looking up. In his mind he was searching for some argument he could use against her.

"It's just a chance," she went on, "a chance dat'll maybe only come once." Lowrie said nothing.

"Whit about dy makkin?" he queried after a while.

Mimie took a mouthful from her fork and chewed.

"I'm tired o makkin. I'm been makkin since I was a bairn, jumper after weary jumper. Besides, we'll no need da money fae dat anymore."

Silence fell on the table. Lowrie was thinking hard behind his stony visage. He thought of asking who would make his meals for him, who would clean the house and do the washing, but realised this might not be the right time. She would be sure to make some remark about his being helpless.

Glancing up, he noticed that she had a certain smugness on her face she wore when she had the beating of him. He said no more.

•••

"Du'll bide wi me, Albert. Promise me du will."

Clemmie, her womb now full to bursting point with a full-grown baby, looked searchingly into the face of her husband. He smiled and nodded, sipped from his glass the whisky he had poured.

"I'll bide," he said in a low intimate voice.

She was scared, and he knew it. She had got the idea into her head that she was too old to be starting a family. He blamed the new district nurse for putting it there.

"It'll be aa right. Du'll see," he reassured her. "An if du wants me to bide to da birth I will."

Clemmie sighed heavily, and moved her position in the sofa, carefully redistributing the bulk of her pregnancy.

"I want de to want it. I don't want de doing it just for me," she said.

"I do want it," Albert stressed, a touch of annoyance in his voice. "Now relax. Don't worry desel."

Clemmie was now one day beyond the expected date. She was tired of carrying this burden about with her. She wanted to have her body back again, to be free.

Albert as promised had arranged leave to coincide with the birth. He'd been home for a week, moving tensely round the house, drinking quite a bit of whisky to counteract the nervous atmosphere.

Life for them had halted. Only the unborn child moved, kicking and elbowing the stomach walls which were no longer a protection but a constraint. The child was ready. Clemmie knew. Albert knew it. It was just a matter of when. And until then, they waited.

Ellen Mary Henry was born at eight minutes past one on the morning of 9th September 1974. She seemed eager to be born, and the birth was without complication. She had thick dark hair and strong lungs.

Albert held her afterwards. His child! He felt a lump rise in his throat.

She was the first baby born to Glimmerwick folk since Lowrie and Mimie's twins. It was quite a time of celebration. Albert drank more than a little whisky.

Clemmie drifted off into a state of emotional euphoria. Relief that the pregnancy was over without mishap transformed into adoration of her child.

What a time it was in Glimmerwick! Even Linda, now very much a fringe figure there, joined in the celebrations.

But all too soon, Albert's leave was over. All too soon, he was picking up the tattered old suitcase that he'd carried with him ever since his first trip, when as a fifteen-year-old, he'd left Shetland for the oceans of the world.

It was on his journey south to the airport that he first noticed all the activity going on in Shetland. For some reason, the significance of North Sea oil had never really struck him before. But now, as he looked out through the sealed glass windows of the airport bus, he felt as if he were a stranger in his own land, a foreigner passing through, watching people alien to him as they busily built new worlds for themselves.

This realisation of his being an outsider was to become an onerous awareness, a knowledge which would gall him more with every trip home he made through the coming years.

•••

The pregnancy was over. It had been long and weighty. But the changes were only beginning.

At Sullom Voe, men and machines began the stripping of the peat layer from the landscape, smoothing and levelling in readiness for industrialization.

A child is born. Seeds sown have germinated and have sprouted. A new life, a new age.

•••

Lowrie eased himself into his chair by the stove-side. He untied the laces on his mud-spattered working boots, and pulled them off. He felt the blood begin to circulate in his feet again.

Mimie was still not home from work at the camp.

He switched on the radio to hear the weather forecast. The plum-mouthed announcer spoke in a monotone voice, following the familiar pattern of forecasting laid out in his script. The forecast for Shetland was stormy.

Since North Sea Oil first hit Shetland six years ago, so much has happened so quickly that events tend to blur, making it difficult to find out just where we're going — or even where we've been. The weight of events pressing upon us tends also to assume a certain inevitability. Where once in the early days of oil we felt fairly sure about the kind of Shetland we wanted, today there is no longer that certainty. The excitement of advanced technology, the illusion of progress, the lure of affluence — all are great eroders of community values, creators of apathy.

JOHN J. GRAHAM,
from the Summer Issue of the
NEW SHETLANDER 1977.

CULTURE CLASH

By 1977, the winding main street of Lerwick was alive with a new electricity. Shorefront pubs were packed with a new clientele. Unfamiliar accents could be heard through the clinking of glasses. The building of the oil terminal was well under way, pulsing out a new heartbeat through the islands, transforming lives. The hotels were full of company reps on expense account stays and skilled tradesmen who were in the islands to perform their specialist tasks.

Accommodation was becoming harder to find. Vacant cottages became valuable assets. Caravans appeared in the oddest of places, rented out for extortionate rates which were met by the big money now flowing from Sullom Voe.

The workcamps were abuzz — huge complexes fitted with every convenience, money no object, full of men recruited from the mainland of Britain and beyond, employed on a month on, week off basis, flown in and out on chartered planes. Their feet barely touched the soil of the islands except that of the terminal — time off was a luxury which was mostly avoided. There was nothing to do anyway. The camps were stationed in the middle of nowhere — the surrounding country was barren. But they were well paid for their efforts. Money abounded, the camp bars were packed every night, illicit gambling sessions commonplace.

Boom time was in full flood, a great river in spate, carrying people along in its furious race downstream. Shetland swelled and threatened to burst under its strain.

Hearing of the well-paid casual work, young people arrived on the *St. Clair* steamer, eager to escape the deepening recession, bringing with them a new street energy, a taste of the punk explosion in the cities. Indigenous youth, reaching out to the new youth culture of the wider world, met them head on. Two cultures clashed, meshed and intermingled. The young began the process

69

of integration, unnoticed by their elders who remained divided for the most part, incomers and locals, separated by an abyss of mistrust.

•••

Lowrie a'Wurlie leaned heavily on his tushkar. He lit a roll-up and paused a while in the midst of cutting the year's supply of peat. The metal blade of his home-made cutter glistened with moisture from within the peat hill, was smeared with fragments of decaying vegetation. Behind him stretched a wall of fresh-cut fuel stacked in brick-like uniformity on the edge of the peat bank, soon to dry in the summer sun, to be carried to the settlement below, and burned in the Rayburn stove at Wurlie.

The bank he was cutting had been in the Manson family as long as they had lived at Wurlie. It was tied to the house with unwritten legality, and contained the kind of peat most highly prized — the bluish variety which would burn as fiercely as any coal.

Each year he cut another two feet of turf to allow extraction. Each year the peat bank moved two feet further from the distant green land below, deeper into the territory of the hare and the curlew. Into the silent high ground, the moors.

Lowrie's inner voice spoke intimately here. Above the immediate world he knew so well, time swung in circles and stopped anywhere he desired — back in the age of the Pict and the Broch, the Celtic time before time.

He was not a religious man. He had no patience with ministers or churches, no love of people when they dressed up in self-importance. But he was a spiritual man, in touch with the rhythmic pulse of his environment, a Celtic man himself.

His inner voice was a murmured one, speaking not with words but with the tiny sounds of nature: the bleating call of a new-born lamb, the bell-tinkling flow of freshwater streams, the rustle of the rising sea wind.

Yet Lowrie had known the full force of the Atlantic blow all his life, had stooped his back in order to continue working through it. He had grasped the soil of Glimmerwick in leathery hands and had kissed it. He was a man made of earth, grown out of it, dependent on it for life.

Like his Pictish ancestors, he saw the invader coming from across the ocean. And like his Pictish ancestors, he was unable, by nature, to resist. He was no warrior. He went on, practising the rituals of his faith, working the land and cutting his peats high above, slow and wise: the rituals of antiquity.

•••

Haggerty handed his ticket to the uniformed seaman at the head of the gangway. The man took the ticket from him and detached the lower portion. He stared at the piece of paper, then directed the traveller to his cabin.

Haggerty picked up his rucksack, took the half-ticket from the hand of the seaman, and entered the reception area of the *St. Clair* passenger ferry from Aberdeen to Lerwick in the Shetland Isles.

A number of narrow corridors ran down the length of the ship to either side of him. He looked at the seaman who was still watching him, to confirm that he was entering the correct corridor, and the seaman nodded.

Down the narrow passage were rows of cabin doors, all numbered in sequence. He walked slowly in the direction given, speaking the numbers under his breath, each one closer to the number he sought.

In his head a rock band played. It was the last tune he had heard on his mother's radio before he left home. It had stayed with him on the train journey north to Aberdeen, always recurring comfortingly just when he thought he'd forgotten it.

He was seventeen and this was his first adventure. Since leaving school he'd been unable to find a job which suited him. The first, as a clerk in a vast office, was a disaster. They wanted him to wear a suit and tie, to be obedient and watchful like a dog, which he was for a while till he saw through the con.

It was all a part of society's conditioning. It didn't end with education, as he'd believed that glorious day when he walked through the wrought-metal gates of the Academy for the last time. Education was only the first step.

Work was the second. He was asked to submit, to give up what made him who he was, to enslave his identity to the company's.

Haggerty had seen it happen to friends of his over the course of the months since they'd left school together, a flock of pigeons freed from their cage. They'd all flown off in different ways. Some had submitted. Others like him had demanded adventure, had gone off abroad or to London with a dream and a rucksack and a quarter of dope.

His only remaining close friend from school was already in Shetland. He'd found a job and a place to stay and had made some friends. Haggerty didn't like following in anyone's footsteps. He rejected Vincent's original invitations to come to Shetland. He wasn't ready then as he was now.

He opened the cabin door and stepped inside. It was empty. He swung his rucksack up onto the top berth and looked out of the porthole. The glass was dull and dirty with the salt spray. All he could see was his own reflection staring back at him, not mirrored, but ghostly with faint shadows from the deck outside showing through his transparency.

He had a broad face. His eyes were set far apart in his head, joined by the curved sheet of bone forehead. His mouth too was wide, like his mother's, except he kept his mostly closed and mute.

At school he'd worn his hair long as a kind of protest, though by the time it had grown to collar length many others had already made the same rebellion.

When he had it all cropped short down to half an inch top and sides, it felt a much more valid protest. No one else wore it like that. He was an original punk, without a label but sharing the anger.

He had an incredible elasticity in his movements. Bones seemed able to bend in his body, all but the flat sheet of curved forehead that sat so prominently atop his face. He was a kind of India-rubber-man, both physically and mentally. He could bend thoughts too, shake them apart like mercury into tiny metallic balls through street-talk and native awareness, then run them together into unity.

He was sure he'd one day do something big. This sojourn to

the north was only a part of some wider plan he had, a stepping-stone, his first adventure. Maybe he would become a popstar, or a painter, or a film director. He didn't know. But he'd do something, one day, or die in the act. No suit and tie for him, no dog-collar. At seventeen, he was his own man, biding his time, awaiting the sign.

Haggerty leapt up onto his bunk, and stretched out. He thought about home, his mother and father, and the dull life of endless repetition they lived. The atmosphere of the house hung over him like a layer of smog, heavy and unclean but oh so normal. He looked at his watch. At this moment, his father would be off to the pub while his mother switched off the radio which sustained her through the day, and switched on the television which sustained her at night.

These thoughts made him glad he'd left. He would concentrate his mind on them. Independence was the key. An adventurer must always look forward.

Then a flashback of dust and tenement blocks, voices in the street and a black cat on a dustbin lid came upon him. He stared down that evening street and found himself walking down it. Yellow lamplight shone over rain-soaked tarmac. Cars and taxis passed him, speeding on the quieter night-time roads.

It was a street from his home, fleeting and familiar, a picture clouded and ill-defined, but one which he instantly recognised. His mercurial mind cast the thoughts up into the air, and they fell as shiny hard balls of thought.

He swept them all together again, digested the feeling and the moment, then turned away from the porthole to where his rucksack lay. In it, on top of his five shirts two jeans seven under-pants ten socks wardrobe, lay a copy of Kerouac's *Dharma Bums*, the paperback edition with the picture of a large golden Buddha smoking a joint on the front cover. He was reading it for the third time.

Beside it, a small blue hardback book which smelled of dust, a book of Zen proverbs he had bought for fifteen pence from a secondhand bookshop.

From a side pocket of the sack, he carefully removed a tiny

pebble of hashish, and climbed up onto his bunk. There, with his back to the cabin door lest anyone should enter, he rolled a small spliff.

When it was complete, he turned to lie with his feet on his pillow, opened the porthole wide, and lit the smoke, puffing the pungent exhalation out through the cracked vent into the harbour air.

It was a kind of air he had not breathed before, a smell of ships and their engines tinged with the salty sea breeze. The smell of a harbour. He sucked it in welcomingly, with a grin on his wide mouth.

"Haggerty's first adventure," he mouthed as the effects of the drug hit him, softening the sharper corners of his splintered adolescent world.

He moved back from the porthole, sat upright on the bunk with his feet dangling down. It was a quarter to six. The steamer would be sailing soon.

•••

At school, Haggerty always had potential. His teachers noted it on his report card with regularity.

But he'd quickly lost interest in academia. He sat a couple of O-grades, passed them, got a job as a clerk.

At work, behind his desk, once he'd got the job down cold, he would sit and visualize the balls and chains round his workmates' legs as they wound their way from desk to desk, exchanging words and papers, or making the inevitable coffee — weak, instant and milky.

He would sometimes write poems, or spend hours through his day pretending to work when he was really drawing a cartoon of the supervisor. It was his escape. He had to. Otherwise his sanity was threatened by being forced to remain in a place he instinctively didn't want to be. He stuck the office job for three months.

Following that, he had a couple of shorter, less demanding jobs, stocking supermarket shelves, pumping petrol.

Before long, he was signing on with most of his mates. But that too was temporary. Soon they all moved on, went their different ways, looking for something, some kind of purpose which would inject positive energy into their lives.

Then only he and Vincent remained, drinking endless cups of coffee through the day, watching television, walking the parks and the art galleries, sitting up late smoking hash, discussing the world and its woes.

They were good times, those. Together they made something complete, a unit primed for learning, reading and digesting the things they needed to know. They bounced books off each other, talked earnestly about their contents, reached earnest conclusions. They pondered art and its relevance to life, philosophised and nodded knowingly. They had a form of love affair, a final glowing of boyish admiration for each other, which made them both feel wanted and necessary.

Then Vincent became very restless. His parents were splitting up again. He felt he couldn't take it. He made plans to go to London, which all fell through at the last moment. Then he heard about Shetland from a friend's older brother and he left, quite suddenly, like a greyhound out of a trap.

Haggerty found himself alone. He spent some time hanging about the old school café, talking to some pupils he had been friendly with, some now studying for higher education, planning ahead for university and college. Their lives had forked apart, on different paths. The things they talked about, he knew nothing of. They still lived in the womb of the peer-group. He was alone. He turned his time to learning.

He read a lot, one book leading to another, as he gradually amassed knowledge. It was a patchy knowledge, quirky and impractical, but one which suited his individuality. If he felt instinctively he didn't care to know something, he could choose to ignore it. And if there was some tangential question that gripped his imagination, he could afford to follow it up. He was his own master.

Living at home with his parents, spending more and more time in his bedroom reading or listening to music or thinking, tension mounted between them. He seemed to notice things about them that had never occurred to him before. Mostly faults and annoying habits that irritated him. He supposed they no doubt felt the same about him. He became sullen and withdrawn, quieter, sadder and more thoughtful.

Feeling some kind of need to express himself on his surroundings, he went out, bought paint off his dole cheque, and began redecorating his bedroom. His mother almost fainted when she saw the colours he had chosen: black and pillar-box red and emerald.

But he spread only a few brushstrokes of hideous-smelling gloss paint before he grew tired of it. He wanted something more permanent.

He wanted to dismantle the whole of his world and rebuild it again, in a shape he understood and enjoyed.

There was a rebellion in him bursting to get out, to break down walls and barriers. But how?

Haggerty lay in his bedroom motionless with the curtains drawn. Pinned to the faded wallpaper above his bed were pin-ups from earlier years — popstars and footballers, beermat souvenirs from his early excursions into pub-life. They stared at him from above, flimsy paper representations of teen-dreams, tinged yellow with sunlight from the time before he drew the curtains.

Around him life moved at its workaday pace. He heard sounds from the street, cars and lorries passing, children playing, drunks at night singing. Everything expressed in familiar patterns of familiar sound. One day he would burst out. One day he would make his rebellious stand. One day he'd have his adventure. . . .

During that period of his life, he became inexplicably emotional. Sometimes he would cry out for no obvious reason, simply overcome by the sense of a sorrow not his own, but shared by all people, a sense of time slipping away unused, of wasted opportunities and bad bets.

He longed for open spaces, for things natural and pure. Yet on the few trips he made to the country, he suffered from a form of agoraphobia, had ached for the tenements to be surrounding him again, setting limits on his vision that he understood.

Then, by chance, he came upon the exit door. In a fit of frustration, he broke the ornate bedside lamp in his mother's room by knocking it to the floor. And those bits of broken lamp, cheap, coarse china, they seemed to make a statement to him.

Form could be destroyed. It could be snapped in pieces. those elements which had been bound together into shapes, in order to create an environment, they were simply crying out to be back in their original forms. Aware of this, he suddenly understood the attraction of precious metals and stones. It was their permanence, their agelessness — immortality.

He realised then that his life didn't have to be any shape in particular. He could do whatever he wanted. He could snap this cage into pieces if he chose to do so.

He wrote to Vincent in Shetland, and began to make plans to leave. He would have his adventure. He would have it now.

•••

That night the *St. Clair* steamer churned a steady northern path through the heaving seas. Haggerty went out on deck and watched as the ship lurched through the night. The salty spray stung his face.

Later in his cabin he was violently sick. The cabin walls creaked and strained, and his head spun round in a dizzy course without pattern.

The smell of his own vomit heightened his sickness. He lay on his bunk wishing he had stayed at home. The hours measured by the digital display of his wristwatch passed painfully slowly.

He was sick and alone, and the feelings of adventurous bravado he had enjoyed earlier in the day seemed far away, still bobbing by the quayside at Aberdeen.

Finally, when his stomach was empty and aching from muscular strain, he fell into a light sleep, soothed by the drone of the engines. He dreamed he was at home, in a record shop he knew, with his mother, of all people.

Together they were thumbing through the records, which were old and their covers dog-eared. Periodically, his mother would pull out a cover and say in an excited voice: "Your dad and I used

77

to dance to this," or some other such comment, as she shoved the tattered sleeve in front of his gaze. In the shop were three attractive girls that he knew, who glanced across at him, giggled and whispered. He wanted to go over to them, to talk, but his mother kept producing another selection of old-favourite-tunes and launching into yet another memory. He felt obliged to stay and listen.

He woke suddenly. It was hot and stuffy and he could smell his own sickness. He turned in his bunk.

In the berth below, another passenger was stirring. He hadn't been conscious of this person entering during the night. His travelling companion stood up and stretched. He was tall and squarely built, with a heavy beard.

Haggerty's eyes shut involuntarily. He began to drift back into sleep.

The movement of the ship was less pronounced now. Perhaps they were in the harbour. Eager to see this place where he would stage his adventure, he overcame his illness and began to dress.

The steamer had slowed in its approach to harbour. It was entering through the south mouth, passing the sheer cliffs of a treeless island, a whitewashed lighthouse on the tip of the island only a stone's throw away.

The land was bare. Yet there were other features that compensated, the flowing colours of the hills and their pronounced shapes. Off the port bow, he could see the shape of a small town unfolding — Lerwick.

The sky overhead was heavy and the sea echoed this greyness. All the contours of the land seemed sharply defined in this unobtrusive light. The town, too, was vivid, a gathering of buildings on a low headland, protruding out from the higher hills inland. He watched as the ship moved slowly north through the harbour till it reached its dock. Here it was moored and the gangway, placed upon the quayside in readiness, connected to the ship to allow passengers to disembark. Haggerty took his rucksack and joined the queue.

He found himself standing next to the man who had shared his cabin. He said 'Hello' politely, but was met with a stiff glare. This

78

reaction puzzled him, but he thought no more of it. He was eager to get off the steamer, to meet Vincent, to explore the early morning town.

•••

The narrow winding main street, Commercial Street, made the first lasting impression on him. He felt as if he had always known it, seemed to remember it from some corner of his past experience.

He walked the street before the shops had opened. It was empty and only a few people passed him. He read the names of the shops as he walked — no chainstores, he noted, small, local businesses.

The twists and turns of Commercial Street seemed to him to be an example of shape suited to fit nature's greater shape, in the way that it followed the line of the coast. He liked it for that reason alone. And he liked the feel of the stone flags beneath his feet.

The day was brightening now. The heavy blanket of grey which had smothered the early sky was splitting into smaller sections, allowing shafts of sunlight to beam down from the blue above. On the upper storeys of the buildings which comprised the main street, he caught sight of the sun and smiled, feeling inside a deep sense of pleasure.

He liked Shetland already.

At lunchtime he met Vincent, who had been working that morning and so was unable to see him earlier. They embraced warmly when they met. Haggerty noticed a nauseating smell rising from his friend which made his mind jerk back to the unpleasant night he had spent on the steamer.

"Christ," he said. "You stink!"

Vincent smiled. "That's what I like to hear, fond greetings."

Vincent explained he had a job labouring in a local fish factory. In the summertime, the factories recruited seasonal staff for the herring. It was smelly work all right, but there were quite a number of students and drop-outs working there. Vincent didn't mind smelling. And he told Haggerty so.

"It's a good crack," he said. "I could get you a job there if you

79

wanted. And a room. That's where I'm staying, in one of the huts."

"Huts?"

"Well, just sheds really, but they're divided up so you have your own room. It's good fun. Lots of girls."

"Girls?"

"Students. Well, most of them."

They went to a shorefront bar Vincent knew, and drank a pint to their reunion. Vincent expanded further on the joys of flinging dead fish about for a living, while Haggerty listened, a little suspiciously.

"It *sounds* ok," he said. "It's just the smell."

"Everybody smells the same, even the girls. So what's the problem?"

Haggerty shrugged. "I could do with a job. I've only got twenty quid."

"Right, it's settled," the fish-worker confirmed, taking a great gulp from his pint glass.

•••

Three days later he joined the sleepy-eyed people trooping through the factory door at eight o'clock in the morning. He was clad in a blue nylon boilersuit Vincent had given him and a long white plastic apron.

The supervisor put him on a machine which washed the fish before they travelled down the line to the filleters. All he had to do was tip boxes of frozen fish from the cold store into the machine. He worked with another man, for two hours, constantly picking up the boxes, walking forward, then emptying them into the mouth of the revolving washer. The machine was like some mythical beast with an endless appetite. No matter how many boxes of fish they emptied into its hungry orifice, it never once halted, nor yet broke wind.

By break-time he was thoroughly sick. Vincent had sold him the job on the promise of girls galore. All he had seen was the back-end of a conveyor belt.

But things improved. In the canteen for fifteen brief minutes, he met some of the promised harem. It was strange, seeing all these women dressed in the same faded pink overalls, and to hear the varying accents emanating out from them. By his side, two old Scottish women spoke in a heavy accent he recognised from his brief stay in Aberdeen, while the girls Vincent was chatting to spoke quite elegant middle-class English. Students, no doubt, as Vincent had said. Haggerty listened without joining in the flirting chatter. He was amazed at his friend's newfound confidence with girls.

Later in the day, the filleters seemed to tire a little, and the rate at which he was expected to turn out the contents of the plastic fishboxes slowed. He had time to stray from his position at the washing machine, and watched the filleters at work with interest. He watched as they cleverly switchbladed the fish, one cut to remove the head, one cut to slit the creature from top to bottom, this carefully behind the skeleton. Then, opening the fish up flat on their filleting board, another sawing stroke removed the backbone. And down the line the unfortunate fish went, to be skinned.

They were a breed apart, the filleters. Around the filleting zone, they moved as if bitten, calling out for more fish, working at high speed, occasionally falling into dispute with the fellow next to them. Sometimes one would step down from his bench and dash to the open factory door, where he would smoke a hurried cigarette while watching the harbour, every minute that passed a fish lost to his wage-packet. While the rest of the workers played out the hours and collected their money, the filleters were plying a skill in return for good rewards.

It was cold in the factory, and as the day closed Haggerty became bored. Again the nauseating smell of fish struck him — but it was as Vincent said, he was growing used to it, and everyone else did smell just the same.

At night, Vincent and he went to a nearby bar. There were other fishworkers there too, some of them the girls he had met that day. But now that they were out of their pink overalls, they seemed so different. In their uniforms, they had seemed like extensions of the same being, the ubiquitous 'packer' stuffing kippers into boxes. But here they all wore the clothes they felt expressed their personality, and were individuals. A few drinks and a lot of happy chatter followed. Haggerty began to relax and join in the conversation.

Two of the group were medical students from Aberdeen University. Two others art students from Edinburgh. Haggerty found himself drawn towards the fifth, a quiet girl, with long dark hair and moonish eyes. She said little, but listened and laughed and enjoyed the company. When one of her friends got up to go to the bar, he switched seats so they could talk.

He discovered that she was a local girl, a Shetlander from the north of the islands. She told him she had just left school and was waiting on news of an application to Edinburgh Art College.

She told him about the hectic time she had had compiling her portfolio, and from the way she spoke, Haggerty sensed that she really respected her talent as a gift.

She spoke with a peculiar accent he hadn't heard before. It was full of 'd' sounds where there should have been 'ths'. He found it quite attractive. While not exactly beautiful, she was definitely pretty. None of her features were perfect, but together they somehow fitted. Her eyes twinkled with a hint of mischief like a child's and at times would glaze over as she spoke, lending her a look of charming vacancy which seemed designed to conceal some inner part of her she wished to remain hidden.

Haggerty carefully guided the conversation round to himself and his adventure. Being in a strange environment, where he was an outsider, it was easy for him to embellish the truth about himself with interesting details which impressed her. His mercurial mind responded to her prompting and he told stories of his past which were plagiarised from books or from the experiences of other people he had heard tell of.

When the lights over the bar went out, and calls of 'Drink up now' echoed round about them, he took her back to his room in the rickety fish hut, and there they made love, on the cast-iron bed under rough woollen blankets, with the lingering smell of fish all around them.

In the morning she was still there, sleeping beside him with her hair tousled, breathing softly. He lay staring at her for a while before she woke. Outside, the seagulls had begun to fight over scraps in squawking skirmishes. Haggerty smiled. He felt good inside. Perhaps this was love, the spur of all adventure he had read about.

He was seventeen.

•••

"Christ, you don't waste any time, do you?" Vincent joked as he rolled a spliff, later. The two friends were sitting by the dockside in a quiet corner, out of sight. The day was almost over. They had finished work, but still wore their fishscale-covered boiler-suits.

"How d'you mean?"

"How do I mean?" he grinned. "You know what I mean, that wee girl last night."

Haggerty smiled.

"Fancy her do you?"

Vincent lit the joint, sucked in a deep breath and nodded slowly, not an eager nod, but an analytical one, holding the smoke fast in his lungs.

"Mmmm . . ."

He passed the spliff to Haggerty, and let out his breath.

"She's ok, but I like the big one better."

It was Haggerty's turn to grin. The 'big one' was at least five inches bigger than his friend.

"Liz?" he scoffed. "Och, she belongs in a different world. Did you not hear her talking about 'mummy and daddy'?" he said, imitating her upper-class accent. "And anyway, she's twice your size."

"We're all the same size in bed," Vincent smiled. "At least, that's what she told me."

Haggerty burst out laughing. "She told you?"

"Yeah, when I asked her how tall she was."

He lay down carefully, with his hands under his head, smiling, watching his friend's reaction.

"And as for her being a snob, that's another thing you'll find out about this place. It doesn't seem to matter where you're from, or what kind of background you've got. Because it's just a summer holiday for most of them, a break from university, they're all just after the same thing, a good time. Well, most of them."

Haggerty laughed out loud. He was beginning to realise that his friend had lost much of his former reticence. He had rebounded to the other extreme. Haggerty wasn't sure if he approved of the change or not. It was difficult for him to remember exactly what form their previous friendship had taken. It didn't seem to matter too much. He sensed that there would be less need for bachelor company here at the fish factory.

As the effects of the joint spread over his mind and body, sensitizing him to the subleties too often overlooked, Haggerty saw Vincent in a different light, not as a boy any more but as the part-completed figure of a man, caught in a state of awkward indecision, covering up his own uncertainty with brash over-confidence.

He suddenly remembered his own exaggerations from the night before, when, fired up with the fuel of alcohol, he had spun stories to the girl he'd spent the night with.

This fleeting realisation of their apparent dishonesty sent feelings of regret shooting through him. It went against all he believed in, his earnest search for truth through Beat and Buddhist dabbling. He stood up, sobered and disconcerted, and without a word went to his little room, while Vincent watched him go with a look of puzzlement on his face.

Haggerty meditated on the matter of his sexuality, lying on his bed consumed in youthful zeal. He wondered if, as men grew out of boys, so they developed some kind of strong polarity, which dictated yearning for feminine companionship to replace their lost sensitivity.

Lying there alone, feeling small and unimportant, he saw a vision of the world as a tiny sphere, spinning wildly out of control until he lost his grip on gravity, and he, like a speck of dust, flew out into space away from everything earthly.

"The meaning of life," he said to his inner self, "is life."

He was seventeen.

Suddenly, his mood was broken by a sharp tap on his door. He heard Linda's voice call his name, and he jumped to let her in.

•••

Summer in the fish factory, processing the boxes of herring that were brought in from the market on the shore, was a season of fevered activity for the vagrant young and holidaying students. From all directions and varieties of background they converged on Shetland in the summer, some saving for the coming terms to augment miserable student grants, some stepping around Europe from casual job to casual job on a kind of quest for meaning in their lives. From Lerwick some would go to pick raspberries or grapes, or to collect dirty glasses in a continental beer festival, while others returned to the portals of academia at university or college.

For a few brief weeks, these very different castes of young folk found their lifelines running parallel. Linda was caught between the two, now assured of a place at art college, but drawn towards the drifting lifestyle Haggerty had chosen for himself.

Their relationship became quite serious. Despite their different backgrounds, they had much in common. He acted as a tutor or guru for her, teaching her much from the individualistic education he had given himself since leaving school.

He taught her about the youth culture of the mainland, its heroes and its myths, gave her a taste of the growing dissatisfaction budding into Punk. He taught her about Burroughs and Kerouac, Richard Brautigan and Tom Wolfe, Henry Miller, Dostoyevski, William Blake, a strange assortment of characters who seemed to him to mirror something of the mood and intonation of his idle days and intense ways. He taught her about Jim Morrison, and Hendrix, Joplin, Dylan. He played her 'God Save the Queen' by the Sex Pistols, the Velvets' 'Heroin', and the Captain's 'Trout Mask Replica'. This and much, much more.

Linda's concept of beauty was changing rapidly. Previously it had automatically been prefixed by 'pretty'. Now it was prefixed by 'power'.

As a person of artistic inclination, it was the revelation that this thinking brought to her appreciation of the graphic arts which influenced her most of all. At school, she had been unable to develop understanding of anything more revolutionary than the Impressionists. Haggerty helped her to appreciate the work of twentieth-century artists, through the same equation of beauty = power harnessed.

It was a difficult concept to grasp. Everything in her conditioning told her that beauty was a summer's day when the sea was at rest, and that the converse of a winter's storm was not only ugly but evil, destroying what the poor folk had struggled so hard to build, taking lives indiscriminately, as it had her father's.

But she was eager to learn. At no point did her appetite for knowledge wane. She overdosed on his ideas. They talked so much that her mind refused to sleep even when she went to bed. She was following the fork in the road and it was leading her further and further away from home.

She unconsciously imitated his style of speech, of dress, of thought. The girl from Glimmerwick was receding deep into her subconscious, living like a hermit in the heart of a colourful forest of new knowledge.

She rarely went home to the bungalow. When she did, she felt imprisoned, longed to be at liberty in the wider world again.

The summer passed slowly.

•••

"I don't like dat boy, Clemmie," Albert frowned, tapping the head of his recently acquired pipe on the arm of his favourite wooden chair.

"Albert, I wish du wouldna do yon. Not on da arm o da chair," his wife replied from her stance in front of the kitchen sink, where she was washing the dishes.

"It's all right, it's out," Albert assured her. "Seriously,

Clemmie, I'm worried about Linda. I hope she's no getting mixed up wi a bad crowd."

This brought little response from Clemmie. She simply turned to look out the window behind the sink, through which she could see her two children playing in the garden. She tapped on the glass furiously, with a look of annoyance on her face, causing a sharp sound to arise, not unlike the sound of the bowl of Albert's pipe knocking on the chair.

"Bide away fae da roses," she shouted, but the children couldn't hear her. She sighed.

"Linda can look after hersel. Believe du me."

"Still," Albert went on, "I don't like dis boy she's taken up wi."

Clemmie shrugged, and rattled plates in the soap-sud-full sink.

"Dere's nothing we can do," she said. "If she's set her mind on something, neither cruelty nor kindness will shift her. She has a terrible, obstinate streak in her, Albert, believe you me."

Albert started repacking the bowl of his pipe, from the small leatherette pouch which formed part of his new-style smoking kit.

"But does du agree?" he asked again.

"About what?"

"Yon boy."

Clemmie glanced through the kitchen window once more.

Her children, Ellen and Isaac, were making mud-pies.

The garden was beginning to fade again. Leaves were withering, blooms had been blown away by the gales of late.

"I don't ken, Albert. It's aa changed since we were young."

"Changed?"

"Everything. Clothes, dancing, even . . ."

"Even what?"

"I don't ken. Attitudes, I suppose."

In the garden, Isaac fell flat on his face in the mud. He started to cry. Clemmie dried her wet hands hurriedly, and flew to the door.

"Inside, both o you," she shouted in a high wavering voice. "Look at da state o you! More dirty clothes to wash! Is it never-ending?"

The children trooped guiltily into the kitchen, covered in slimy wet mud.

87

"It wasna my fault," Ellen protested, "he just fell."

Clemmie ignored her defence, and herded them both through to the bathroom, where she made them wash and change.

Albert was left alone in his resting-chair, his favourite chair. It had belonged to his father and his grandfather before that. He lit his pipe and sucked on it thoughtfully.

It seemed that during his last trip to sea, Clemmie and Linda had fallen out irrevocably, but Clemmie refused to tell him any of the details, other than that Linda had been cheeky and rude, and had hurt her.

The day before, a Saturday, he had met Linda and her new boyfriend by chance, on Commercial Street. They exchanged only a few words, hardly meeting at all, but Albert had sensed something about the boy that disturbed him. He had the feeling he had seen the face before but couldn't place it. Perhaps it had been at a railway station or an airport, perhaps they had walked past each other, fixed eyes as strangers do and held each other's histories in that contact. Whatever, he was certain he had seen him before.

There was something in the boy's face that worried Albert. At sea, where the crews were constantly changing, and of all nationalities, Albert had seen that look before: the glazed look of marijuana.

He didn't dare tell Clemmie what he suspected. She would have eaten herself away had she known. It was better if he could gently apply pressure, so that Linda gave up the boy before she became involved.

Soon, she would be leaving Shetland for art college, and would be independent of them. She would have money of her own from her time at the fish factory and a grant from the government. He was glad in a way, although he loved the girl. He understood now what a terrible strain she had been for Clemmie of late. She no longer came home regularly and when she did, she just seemed to sleep all the time. Clemmie had her hands full with the children now. Linda was an extra burden.

But he would make sure she was all right before she left. It was his responsibility

•••

Haggerty was through with the fish factory. It was a cold, dirty job with no future. He hated having to work there, and resented getting up in the morning to don his fishy clothes again. His mind began to work on the matter of Sullom Voe and how he could cut a slice of its big money for himself.

Linda had noticed his growing dissatisfaction and was flattered to think that it might have something to do with her leaving for college. But she knew him well enough by now to realise that there was more to it than that alone. Maybe it was because the summer was nearly over, and the holiday spirit rapidly disappearing with it. Many of the students had already left in order to prepare for the coming term.

She wasn't sure of her feelings for him. Certainly she felt a strong urge to be with him, certainly they had something strong and good. But he could be cruel too.

Often he would deride her naivety, mock her for being a simple country girl till she lost her temper with him. And when she did, a smug self-satisfaction melted over him as if he had done what he had set out to do.

"I'd like to have a croft," he announced one lunchtime in the canteen of the factory, after they had sat for half an hour eating in silence.

Linda looked up in surprise.

"A croft? What for?"

Haggerty pushed a piece of steamed pudding round the cracked plate in front of him.

"Animals and things, cows and sheep and chickens. I'd like to . . ."

Linda couldn't supress her amusement. She burst out laughing. Haggerty frowned and looked serious.

"Dat takes money," she stressed, adopting his mood, "and how'll you get money if you stop working here?"

"I could get a job at Sullom Voe," he said, as if he had been insulted by her tone.

"You can't get a job till you've got an address. Dey won't take you on if you haven't got somewhere to live. You can't put 'c/o da Fish Factory' on your application form."

He pushed the plate of pudding away from him and shook his head.

"Can't get a job without an address. Can't get an address without a job. Christ, this is supposed to be a bloody oil boom, we're supposed to be making our fortunes. Oil boom, capital 'O' capital 'B', for christsakes!"

He glared round the bare canteen which had never been lined, at the corrugated iron roof and mass concrete walls.

"Look at this shit-hole!" he groaned. Linda gave a short nervy laugh. She was tired of his moaning.

"It's all right for you to bloody laugh, you're off to your goddamn college. It's me who's staying," he went on.

She felt a little sorry for him then. It was true what he was saying, she did have something to anticipate, while his future was empty.

A tense silence followed. At a nearby table, a group of filleters had overheard them and were laughing. Linda blushed. Haggerty glared at them fiercely. By now they had lost all novelty for him and were no longer romantic as they had first seemed.

"What about that house you told me about, the one you used to live in?" he said sharply to Linda.

"In Glimmerwick?"

"Yes, in Glimmerwick. Where else?"

"But it's right next door to my auntie," she gaped.

"Couldn't you arrange for me to rent that? Then I could get a job at Sullom Voe. You could go off to art college and we'd both be happy."

"Oh no, you couldn't, no right next door to dem."

"Why not? If you arranged it, maybe I could get it cheap."

As the shock faded, she realised that he was serious. What could she do? Clemmie made no secret of the fact that she disapproved of Haggerty. Only the week before, she and Linda had staged the most outrageous scene over him, when Clemmie had laid it on the line to her that he was a bad influence.

Linda was amazed at Clemmie's attitude. She hardly knew Haggerty, and was acting completely out of character. Normally her aunt believed the best about people till they proved her wrong.

It was not until after many angry words were exchanged that the reasons were revealed. It was Albert's fault as usual. He'd told her he believed that Haggerty was taking drugs, and that she should try to intervene before Linda was hurt.

Linda had laughed. She really laughed, at their naivety and narrowmindedness. She told her aunt that she was right, that Haggerty did smoke 'hash', that she had tried it herself and that it was no worse than drinking. Something Albert himself did plenty of.

Clemmie became hysterical, and Linda ended up walking out, telling herself that this was the last time. She wouldn't listen to anymore of their antiquated notions. It was her life from now on.

And now Haggerty was trying to enter into the very world she had rejected in favour of his! There was a very real irony in it all, life had doubled back on her and caught her from behind, like a bogey-man springing out of nowhere, or the man in the lane looking up.

Days drifted past. She hoped that Haggerty would forget his idea, but he didn't. He kept on pestering her about it, asking if she had spoken to her aunt about the house, till finally she thought she would go mad. Instead of nipping the whole scheme in the bud, that first day in the canteen, she let it all slide by, hoping it would go away, until now it had grown so big and so weighty that it pinned her down. Her own dreams and ambitions became secondary to his. Art college no longer seemed important. He was using the croft in Glimmerwick as a form of blackmail made desperate because she loved him, and had given up her home and family in favour of him.

She wondered if he knew. If it was all a game for him, a further expansion of the baiting game he played sometimes with her. He seemed to be exerting some kind of force over her, at every turn mastering her, and so insulting her. The hurt went deep and stayed there.

He refused to discuss art college with her. When she brought the subject up, he simply said that, in his opinion, all that college would do for her was to teach her to do the same things as everybody else.

"You could do better teaching yourself," he would say, almost scornfully, closing the subject with a gesture of disinterest.

Linda knew that she could never go back to her aunt and do as Haggerty wanted, she couldn't beg her aunt to help them. For one thing, Clemmie would have refused. Finding an alternative became imperative. Her head was spinning.

She didn't know how she felt about anything any more. She wanted to go away for a while, somewhere new, a place where she was a stranger, yet the fear that no one would care or be there when she came back prevented her. Art college loomed closer. Days in the fish factory seemed such a waste of time. But what could she do? One way or another, she had to lose.

It was a Sunday in late August. A spell of wet and windy weather had broken and the air was warm and still. A light sea fog had settled over the islands, clouding the hills of Bressay out of sight. In Lerwick harbour, the water moved imperceptibly, slapping the stone of the dockside with a gentle rhythm.

The two young lovers walked down to Victoria Pier in the afternoon, and strolled around looking at the ships which were harboured there. They bought sweets from the little shop at the pierhead, and threw bits to scavenging seagulls. Neither spoke. There was a heaviness between then, an indecision which divided them, over their relationship and their direction, whether mutual or individual. Soon it would have to end. She would have to decide.

In the small boat harbour, an expensive yacht lay with its sails tucked neatly away, resting. Haggerty examined it carefully. On the opposite side of the harbour, about thirty yards away, lay a row of Shetland Model boats, once integral to the Shetlanders' livelihood, but now used exclusively for pleasure. Some Sunday afternoon sailors were pottering about.

Haggerty watched them with an expression of distaste. Linda watched him. She knew that there would be a comment.

"Bloody Vikings, aren't they?" he said at last. "All this nonsense about Norse ancestry, Up Helly Aa Fire Festivals, roots," he went on, mocking the sailors and their boats.

Linda said nothing. She sat down on a black metal bollard on the edge of the pier, broke a cube of chocolate from the bar in her hand, and popped it into her mouth. Her mind suddenly cleared and she felt aware of some special understanding previously denied her. She looked carefully at the men as they lovingly handled their boats and sailing gear, and was reminded of her Uncle Albert in Glimmerwick, who was so pernickety about his boatshed. He was forever coiling bits of rope and reorganising this or that. He was worse than Clemmie with her house. The two of them were so obsessed with getting everything just right that neither of them ever really did anything.

She drifted off into one of her trances. Haggerty looked down at her where she sat, staring vacantly into the water, and wondered about the motions of her mind. What did she think of, all those times when she sat doing nothing, gazing into space? Where did she go all those hours she spent half-asleep?

Linda was realising for the first time how she had changed. She had become a different person from the one she was intended to be. It had happened slowly over a number of years, so slowly that she had hardly been aware of it. But now the feelings came back, of being invaded by another being, and she heard quite clearly the footsteps of the man in the lane as he passed by her window.

Suddenly a shutter dropped in her mind, cutting the memory off. She started, her trance broken. Haggerty smiled. She stood up and took him by the arm.

"You're right," she said, "they are bloody Vikings."

Haggerty laughed; he didn't understand the significance of those words. He didn't know that they symbolised Linda's uprooting. He was too intent on finding his own way to puzzle over her patterns.

Shetland had changed him. In the course of that summer spent working in the fish factory, he had realised for the first time how it felt to be an outsider. He'd become something of a local character, well known for his tattered appearance and spiky haircut. People had noticed the strange youth, talking with adolescent authority to the followers he had accumulated. He had become something of a cult figure.

But he didn't want disciples. Although he never admitted to

93

his insecurity publicly, he was being weighed down by these hangers-on who had attached themselves to him. He had nothing to give them, no wisdom, no encouragement. All he could give was criticism. Yet still they waited on his words as if they were manna, enjoying his criticism, thriving on the hurt. It was as if he acted as a release for them, letting out the guilt they felt as a result of changes going on within them — the guilt of adolescence, when the oh-so earnest search for truth and purpose disappears in the morass of adult ego.

All this he considered fair enough. But where was his release? Who performed that function for him, except Linda?

He never set out consciously to hurt her. He cared for her. But there were times when he exploded, when she spoke thought-lessly, not from her intellect but from her powerful Shetland background, rounding off life's perplexities with some pithy aphorism handed down to her from older generations.

There was a strong instinctive side to her with which he could never identify. And when she showed that dark side to him, he felt as if she was trying to shut him out.

But he really did care for her. There were times when she dressed in a vacant beauty not unlike the stillness of a windless day in Shetland. She might stand silently for half an hour, looking at nothing in particular, in a kind of trance. This ease of relaxation he found well nigh impossible.

He was prone to bitterness, a sour gut feeling that screwed ever tighter into itself, till his temperament became brittle like glass. His mercurial mind still held the shiny metallic balls of thought, but they were scattered and so its power was dissipated.

He was becoming more defensive with people, more critical. He could strike out with sharp words, as Linda well knew, he could hurt.

The bitterness was swelling and filling him. His Dharma-Bum-Zen philosophy was breaking up and splintering.

•••

So she had gone the other way! He had feared as much. He

94

folded the letter carefully and placed it in his wallet. Later he would file it in the desk of his cabin along with the others that bore the same spidery writing — Clemmie's.

The sun forced a blinding globe through Albert Henry's half-shut eyes and his beard itched in the heat. He was tempted to shave it off until his next leave. From the bridge of the ship he surveyed the deck below. The tanker would cross the Equator in five days. It was a trip he had made many times before and it no longer filled him with any great thrill. Three members of the Malaysian crew wandered between the valves and pipes below, checking for faults or gas leaks. He watched them disinterestedly, his mind far away in Glimmerwick, puzzling over Linda and how they had lost her somehow. Albert's feelings for his niece went deeper than he liked to admit. He saw much of Clemmie's lost girlishness in her and was disturbed by their falling out, to the point of restless nights. He dreamt one clammy tropical night that they two, Clemmie and Linda, merged into one being, that he made love to them both in silence and that they split forever separate afterwards: though they remained one being. That Clemmie was rejecting herself in Linda. The tense cords that bound their lives together gripped his throat in the form of choking heat. He longed for a cold northern wind to blow on his face. But she had chosen the other way.

He had feared this path not only for Linda, but for Shetland as a whole. The path of affluent lure, the way of oil. At times it all seemed inevitable. Wasn't he himself dependent on it for his livelihood now, here on board this supertanker with its black cargo?

In the early days he had advocated resistance as vital, albeit belatedly, long after the first battle of propaganda was well won by the multinationals. Now he was ever more inclined to the view that there was only one weapon remaining, to scran as much as possible, to grasp the fringe wealth offered, to fight a war of grab. A token gesture, a bitter one.

In the course of Albert's imagined war, he had become possessed by a fierce-jawed demon. Perhaps a chromosome or two of Viking still active in him. He was an exiled rural guerrilla monitoring the course of his imagined war through the local paper and the letters from his friends, mapping strategies of wasp-sting strikes at the enemy.

But he was late again. The changes had already begun to gel in their sculpted moulds. The new Shetland, although featureless, was a complete embryo — unveiled but alive and breathing through straws of integration peeping through from the subsoil to the clean air above. Its nursemaid, the god of sudden change, stood guard.

Big Money

Mimie a'Wurlie had taken a job as a chambermaid at Firth Camp. In the mornings, Sundays too, she rose at half-past five while Lowrie slept on. It was the first period in their married life when she riddled and coaxed the daily fire of peat.

Firth Camp where she worked accommodated around 1,100 men, all employed in some capacity on the building of the oil terminal — welders and fitters, plumbers and electricians, engineers and managers, plus the caterers who cooked their food and washed their plates, cleaned their toilets and made their beds. A mixture of people from a variety of backgrounds all hungry for money at a time when it was scarce.

A mixture — conmen and Christians, drunkards and dopeheads, ex-seamen and soldiers. Irish and Scots pre-dominantly, with a fair percentage of Englishmen, especially in the managerial positions, and a sprinkling of other characters from further afield. Some big and gentle, some small and mean. But mostly in between.

Their days were spent on site and their nights were often long. They worked overtime and overweekends, when the money was even better. But wives and children, families waited over the sea. Some turned to drinking, some left after a few weeks. Some stuck it out and earned the big money, but suffered in other ways. Some stayed, not only for the money but for the boom-time spirit itself, getting high on the energy generated by industry rushing forward and its thrilling slipstream. And some stayed for Shetland, a few who managed to escape the confines of the company, to reach out to the real Shetland outwith oil, to walk the silent moorland and the clifftops. A mixture of men.

The camp itself had been hastily manufactured out of short-life materials, and was destined to be dismantled when the boom was over, like its still bigger sister at nearby Toft.

It was a vast complex of luxury portacabins linked together by endless lengths of corridor, each block containing a number of box-like rooms, furnished with the essentials of suitcase living.

At the heart of the complex lay the giant canteen and kitchen, where teams of white-suited men prepared mountains of food and threw half out when the meal was over. Despite the staggering waste, the taking of left-overs was strictly illegal.

Each morning, fleets of red buses trimmed with rusting chrome moved in convoy towards the site. Many hangovers made that early morning journey, heavy heads, dreaming about home, transported in vehicles still bearing notice of their one-time destinations in Lowland Scotland, when their chrome had been shiny and new: Falkirk, Kilsyth, Bridge of Weir, Linlithgow, names which were like small flags of belonging for many of the men, in a strange alien place.

At the airstrip nearby, now refurbished after years of dereliction following the departure of the wartime forces, aircraft roared their engines and plunged up and downwards through the clouds, taking men home for their leave, bringing them back for another month's work. In the harbour, two small liners lay permanently moored as accommodation for the more senior staff who required greater comforts.

On site, solid buildings began to replace huts and cabins. Roads were tarmaced and blueprints moulded the land. The sea of mud took concrete form. The end was still a long way off, but so too now was the beginning.

In the evening, the same fleet of buses made the return journey, ferrying the men to their camps which had been cleaned and readied through the day by legions of cleaners. Huge vats of soup steamed, steaks waited their turn on the conveyor belt of hunger.

After dinner, bars bulged. The camp became an alcoholic paradise. Glasses were drained and refilled, a constant quenching process stretching from opening time till closing time and beyond.

It was boom time. Big money, high times. Few were free of the narcotic pull. Much of the big money never left Sullom Voe. It simply passed from the hand of the employer through the employee into the hand of the caterer. Wage packets were ripped open on Friday and never closed till they were badly tattered.

To begin with, Mimie was one of the few who resisted the urge to spend.

She had a firm purpose for her money. (Canada!) She ignored the baubles of material wealth now dangling within reach. Friday meant another hundred pounds towards her target figure, and her dream was becoming a reality.

But in time her attitudes changed. While her job was routine and dull, her environment most certainly was not. She had one or two shocks coming to her. Shocks administered to her unintentionally by people unaware of her naivety, but shocks just the same. She saw many things for the first time. Idle violence, vandalism, loose prostitution, drugs. She tried to shut her eyes to it all.

It was her friendship with one of the freed-from-the-closet homosexuals which brought to her an understanding. Her gay acquaintance, a barman whose room was one of those which Mimie cleaned, would often come to chat to her through the day when he was off work. He would chatter to her while she hoovered and polished, in a dainty effeminate voice which roused a reaction of humour from the crofter's wife; sometimes he helped with the work if she had fallen behind schedule. He knew how to clean all right!

During the sixties he had been a dancer in London. He had been married then and had a daughter, now ten years old. He told her a great deal about the 'crazy times', as he described them, and the 'bad scenes' he had been through. Mimie didn't say much to begin with, simply chuckled to herself. But in time she came to realise that these people she had looked on as so alien were no other than herself, that their strangeness was not inherent but of another culture — a rich one where folk could be different from one another.

Through all that her new friend told, Mimie recognised the omnipresent figure of his mother and knew that she in some way acted as a surrogate. This relaxed and strengthened their alliance. Mimie fulfilled his expectations.

She took him home to Glimmerwick for tea. Lowrie gaped while he chattered. The old crofter uttered not one word besides 'aye aye' and 'goodbye'.

Mimie laughed to herself. She like to see Lowrie lost for words. And she liked Jimmy, her gay acquaintance, and knew that he withstood tremendous pressure from the other men at the camp.

When he was dismissed for being found in another man's bed, she was truly sad. They bade each other a tearful goodbye while he waited for the flight which would take him 'doon the road'. When he was gone, she thought of him going back to the nice house he had bought for his mother, out of work and defeated.

But there was always someone else. Always someone on her corridor helpless, always someone to replace the last. Perhaps to replace her own children now out of reach? Perhaps. She made a habit out of fostering the lost souls who weren't coping with the pressure of long-term contract work. Particularly the younger ones, away from home for the first time.

She saw many things for the first time. But she came to know that the purveyors and the users of these vices were just people who had lost their way. She knew it and tried to help. Lowrie told her to stop. He said she'd be hurt, that she was too soft, that sooner or later one of her wards would wound her just for spite, because they knew they would get away with it.

But she went on. She was being drawn into the Sullom Voe vortex, into its bubbling force field. She resented Lowrie nagging at her all the time. He had been against the oil from the very start, ever since the Haa House was gutted and left. Of course she knew the reason, she knew how strongly attached he had been to that building. It had been a part of his life as long as he had lived. But even so, he could hardly be termed rational about oil. He spoke as if it would take from the islands without giving back anything in exchange. But Mimie's bank book said differently.

Somewhere along the merry road from Glimmerwick to Sullom Voe, Mimie's attitude to money had changed as well. Acquisition was now paramount and her objective secondary. She imagined herself saving enough money to holiday in Canada, not simply once, but whenever she chose. Then she would have it all —

Lowrie happy on his croft with his feet firmly in the ground while she jet-setted out to Canada to see her twin sons. Money could buy this for her. She understood now. Mimie knew.

So she suspended her trip and worked all the overtime she could. The hundreds in her bank book became thousands, and she grew stouter and sunnier and redder. Her doctor in Hillswick warned her of the dangers of high blood pressure and the strain which this placed on the heart.

But she went on, puffing and sweating day after day, rising at half-past five to catch the minibus to work, cleaning and polishing with vigour grown from greed.

In the crofthouse of Wurlie, Lowrie waited. He was worried. He knew the girlish smiles that hid the strain and knew that she was clinging onto something which would finally pull away and shrug her off. What would she do then, even if she had her health?

There was little he could do. She had an answer for everything. If he mentioned blood pressure, she laughed it off.

"I ken my body better dan any doctor. I'll ken when I've to stop, Lowrie."

What could he do but wait? He did his work about the croft as he'd always done, but the atmosphere was different now. Before Sullom Voe, his days had seemed so full. Now, even though he did far more around the house, peeling the potatoes for dinner and cleaning up, now they were empty. Years before, he had seen the house change when his parents died. Then once again when his children left. But he had always thought that Mimie would be there, he had relied on that fact for a reason to carry on.

Only his dog Nell cared for his loneliness. Even the sheep and the hens seemed unmoved. Glimmerwick had become fragmented and splintered. Its once sealed-in soul was gone.

He wandered about with Nell at his heel, smoking and scanning the ocean like an ancient Pictish sentry. But the shadowy shapes of passing tankers and drilling rigs beyond stayed out of sling-shot. He was powerless. His life too had become a shadow, thin and formless, dependent on the presence of others for its vitality.

His only consolation lay in the unchanging land. Only it went on as before, growing and dying. Its colours were as old friends whose hands he could never shake but whom he could nod at from a distance. He would stand on the shore and linger while the salt spray rose on blasts of wind and stung his leathery old face; he would grin. He would watch the light fade and dawn and lie awake while Mimie snored another tiring day into her past, wondering.

His question was the same in 1979 as it had been in 1973.

"Tinks du will it ever be da same again?"

Will it ever be the same again? There is only ever one answer and Lowrie knew it. He was well acquainted with change — and hated it.

SOOTHMOOTHERS

The tiny one-roomed Post Office near the voehead, on the road to Glimmerwick, had come to life of late. In the hands of Winnie, now known to all as 'Winnie oda shop', and her husband who had a shift job at Sullom Voe, it had sprouted new shelves right to the roof full of tinned and packet foods; it now supplied, paradoxically, milk and bread to the crofting community round about, twice a week when the Lerwick bus came north.

It was hardly a lucrative business. Had it not been for the sub-postmistress's salary, perhaps they would have thought twice about buying the business over. But Eshaness, like the rest of the north mainland, had come alive since the boom began. Old crofts once doomed to dereliction were occupied by young couples, many of them from 'da sooth' (there was a certain conflict between the new crofters' methods and those of the old — Jerusalem Artichokes versus kail and tatties). New houses had burst out of barren land, fertilised by oily affluence. Not that many of the newcomers patronised Winnie's shop — most of them were too health conscious to eat the kind of preservative-ridden products on her shelves. But it was a nice sideline for Winnie now that her children were all at school in Lerwick. The shop was most often empty and she spent her time sitting on top of the paraffin heater reading other people's magazines, while the warm oily fumes rose up the rear of her nylon overall — her favourite roost, from where she would flutter forward periodically fanning the tails of her garment with a full-cheeked blaw.

A little bell tinkled on the door of the Post Office when a customer entered. Winnie hid the schoolteacher's copy of *Practical Knitting* under the counter, carefully so as not to damage it.

A tall thin woman dressed in a plastic raincoat entered, and closed the latch-lock door behind her. She unfastened the hood of her coat, and shook the drops of rain from her hair and face. She had an attractive freshness in her complexion, without the native ruddiness grown from sea gales.

"Good morning," chirped the postmistress. "Wet da day."

Her customer nodded, and tried to smooth the rumpled stems of her umbrella.

"Yes," she replied, "and windy too."

"You'll be wanting your papers, Mrs Glossop. *Radio Times* and *Observer*, isn't it? You're da only ones hereabouts dat takes da *Observer*, you ken."

Winnie's remark was double-edged. It was designed to show she knew her customer's needs, and also, just a mite mischievously, to point out the difference between incomers and local folk. She fetched the papers from their shelf.

"You'll have heard young Andrew's coming home?" she asked as she laid them on the counter.

The tall woman shook her head.

"No?" she replied, not knowing who 'young Andrew' was and not really caring.

"Your neighbour's son, Andrew, da doctor." The postmistress leaned forward over the counter. "Da one dat Mimie a'Wurlie's always bragging o."

When this disclosure too failed to kindle any familiarity between them, Winnie oda shop gave up. She had tried on a number of occasions to rouse Barbara Glossop to gossip, each time without success. Winnie was a little peeved by this. She normally allowed others to come to her with their news, and conducted the exchange from the paraffin heater. With Mrs Glossop she spent her time leaning over the counter trying to engender intimacy.

The tall customer packed her newspapers in the straw bag she carried, withdrew her purse and handed a one pound note to the postmistress. Winnie put the pound in her till and handed over coins. Business! Mrs Glossop placed these coins in her purse and turned to leave. She stepped towards the door, then hesitated.

"I don't suppose you've a loaf of fresh bread?"

"No," said Winnie, "none till da morn's night fae Lerwick."

•••

That day, the rain cleared in the afternoon and a light breeze chased gloom beyond the purple heather hills of August. At night the summer sun moved slowly to rest, unobstructed, till it hovered over the western ocean in a blaze of colour. Barbara Glossop walked from her house down to the shore beneath Glimmerwick and stood watching the sky.

"Gold," she said, her eyes fixed on the perfect round of the setting sun.

"Oil," he had said, her husband, eagerly. "Where there's oil there's gold." She hadn't known then that she would find real gold. The city seemed a long way off.

"Goats!" he had said, their neighbour Lowrie the crofter, tightlipped, watching as they began the stocking of the land from the rickety van which had carried them north over motorway and ferry, double-track and single-track roads, till it wound home to Glimmerwick. She laughed.

"Soothmoothers!" he had said, bitterly, from the new bungalow across the turning place, their landlord, Albert Henry, the same man who grasped their money every month with stone-faced displeasure. She didn't understand them.

"Integration," he had said, warmly, the fresh-faced community worker, himself a soothie, just out of college and his head packed full of sociological theorising. She had said little — his words would change nothing — people were real, not statistical.

"Gold," she murmured again and turned away from the shore as the final thinnest arc of glistening light dipped out of sight, leaving its beauty as an imprint of fading colour on the clear sky. She shivered a little as she walked back to her home, their little crofthouse tucked under the steep rising peat hill behind, looking as if it had always been there, as if it would always be there, as if it should. Its home-fashioned design was as insistently perennial as the docks which she tried so hard to uproot from her garden.

She had been reluctant to move to Shetland, although her husband had worked at the oil terminal for some months, as a resident of the camp at Firth prior to moving. It represented a sweeping change to her lifestyle.

From the Midlands to the north land. From suburbia to Glimmerwick. From modern day, into a slower older time.

She fell in love with the croft on first sight. The sea at the bottom of the garden, the views across the ocean. Though the winter there had been difficult to say the least, the summer was worth while. Only their relationship with their neighbours disturbed her, or rather the lack of it, for despite living within a stone's throw of one another, rarely did they speak more than good-day.

That first word Albert Henry uttered, 'soothmoothers', then a set of syllables without meaning, now burnt a hole inside her when she thought of it. The syllables had a sharp cutting edge of steel, which Albert Henry used with skill. Her husband Eric called it outright hostility, but Barbara was less certain. She saw her neighbours as folk who felt threatened, they and their traditions, by oil and incomers. As folk pressed back against a wall of time, hiding behind it. The first steps were the hardest. The eventual product was a blend, a merging. Why then did this process have to be so prolonged, made so painful by both sides?

"Gold," she said again as she entered the porch of the house. But it was only a memory now and sadly transient.

•••

Next morning, Barbara Glossop rose early, as her husband was preparing to leave for work. She looked out the tiny window of her but room. A thick fog had settled over the bay of Glimmerwick and was lying heavy on the water. There was no wind at all. She smiled and kissed her husband's cheek as he left.

After breakfasting, she went out into the garden, armed with a spade and a pair of gloves, ready to begin another round of the sporadic wrestling match she conducted with the docks. It was easy to pull away the growth above the soil. It was the yellowish root which remained that gave battle.

She had been in the garden for some minutes before she noticed the shiny saloon car at the side of the Mansons' house.

Some time later she was aware of someone standing watching

her. She looked up. This, she deduced, was the son who had done well for himself.

"Tough, aren't they?" he said in an accent which had little of the native intonation left in it, from beyond the stone dyke.

"Yes," she replied with a smile, standing up.

He vaulted the low dyke with agility, and stood beside her. He offered her his hand.

"I'm Lowrie's son, Andrew. I'm home from Canada for a few days," he explained with a hint of the Americas in his voice.

At close range she found it difficult to assess him. His outright friendliness came as a shock, in a place where she had grown used to solitude. She took off her tattered gardening glove and they shook hands.

He stayed with her for a while, in the garden. He was very talkative, eager to know all about Barbara and her husband, how they had come to Shetland, why, where from. His mannerisms and speech did not betray his origins, the fact that he had spent his childhood here in Glimmerwick. His rapid chatter reminded her of a city street, busy, very busy, but the words, like pedestrians, travelled in their own directions.

"My father tells me you keep goats?"

"Your husband works at Sullom Voe, I hear?"

"And you've settled here in Glimmerwick ok?"

She answered his questions thoughtfully, with a certain respect for the fact of his roots here in Glimmerwick. She wondered if he was sent as some kind of emissary from Wurlie.

Only once did the tempo slip. In that pause, the doctor from Canada looked around him at the fog-laden bay and the hills surrounding, and as he did so she caught sight of a look which contained something less than certainty. For a moment, she expected him to cast a wide-flung gesture to the horizon and eulogise, to say something like "All this could have been mine".

Ultimately, he said nothing. He bade her a cheery goodbye and vaulted back over the dyke to the no-man's land of the tarmac turning place.

But she sensed it. She noticed that trace of pique in his face as he left, at the fact that he couldn't have everything — his life in Canada and his home.

As she watched him walk towards Wurlie, clad in his well-cut suit, she caught herself muttering, "Soothmoother . . .".

He had done well for himself, if steps on the social ladder were your chosen measure. But nothing is gained without loss, compensatory reaction to action. What he had lost, she had gained. Here in Glimmerwick she had found a home, not a house as they had lived in on the mainland. She would stay. This was her place now — she was a Shetlander.

•••

"Bread," she said, with purpose in her voice. Eric was asleep by her side and stirred as she spoke. Barbara smiled and lay down next him. She shook her pillow loosely.

The very stuff of life. The ingredients must be thrown together and stirred, blended and allowed to swell and rise, kneaded and allowed to rise — long before baking.

"Integration," he had said, enthusiastically, with a finger running over the grain of the clean corded trousers which he wore, the young social worker she had mocked in her mind. But perhaps she had been too hasty. Maybe it *was* a little like baking bread, a slow gentle firmness in the kneading being necessary.

It was the place which mattered, not the people and where they came from, what they called themselves, what they did. The islands would remain long after oil.

That night she thought it all out. By morning, she knew what to do. When Eric left for work, she brought out her baking bowl and began. By lunchtime, she opened the oven door on her Raeburn stove and pulled out two moist pound loaves of hot fresh rye bread.

"Integration," he had said, her community worker, as if the word alone was enough to bring about the changes, as if the theory would leap out of his textbooks and mould people.

"Bread," she said, at the door of the bungalow. "I was baking and I thought you might like a loaf."

Clemmie Henry stammered. She hesitated. The children were out and Albert was at sea. The house behind her hid nothing.

"It's rye bread," Barbara Glossop said, with a slow gentle firmness in her voice.

"Ja," said Clemmie smiling, taking the offered gift. "Would you like a cup of tea?"

The very stuff of life.

•••

Glimmerwick found a new heart. It was Barbara Glossop's. Her love for the place touched everyone. She was cheerful, she wore bright clothes, she laughed.

She became friendly with Clemmie and with Lowrie a'Wurlie, though Lowrie never fully released the growl from his voice when she spoke to him.

Clemmie grew to trust her new neighbour and confided in her. She unburdened herself completely: Linda, Albert, the children, her loneliness — everything.

Barbara Glossop listened and sympathised and encouraged Clemmie to be more selfish. They were roughly the same age, yet Clemmie seemed to her to be so much older — perhaps it was to do with her marrying so young, and taking on the responsibility of her niece when she was little more than a child herself. Barbara's own history was so different. She had been to university in the late sixties and had travelled around Europe as a student before settling down to a career in wine importation, a line she had followed right up until she moved the Shetland with her husband. In England, she had been a suburban hippy cultivating her vegetable patch and baking bread and voting Labour, and had missed the security of that lifestyle when she moved. But not any more. She was giving something now.

Something worthwhile. And subconsciously she knew it. And when she met Linda, and found herself acting as a kind of catalyst, bridging the gulf between aunt and niece, trying to explain and understand simultaneously.

Linda was living with her boyfriend in a caravan and had found a job at Firth Camp, cleaning like Mimie a'Wurlie. She had not taken up the place offered to her by the art college. Clemmie could not accept this. The breach seemed permanent.

Barbara tried to draw them together again, with a little success. Clemmie respected her friend's judgement, and listened when she spoke of the need for people to choose their own direction in life, when they themselves are ready, not when society dictates. She listened while Barbara told her that she had smoked hash herself as a student, and that there was no medical evidence to suggest that it was any more harmful than alcohol. She listened as she told her of a former boyfriend, an Australian, with whom she had hitchhiked around Yugoslavia and Italy, who had been classified as 'bad company' by everyone from her mother to her best friend.

"Linda's just experimenting, Clemmie," she would say. "Give her time . . ."

Clemmie did. It was all she could give. She couldn't muster any strong feelings any longer, not for Linda, nor Albert, and at times not even for her children. She was consumed with the fear that she had somehow missed out on her youth, and that it was now too late to rectify this. The more cheerfully Barbara spoke of her own full youth, the more subdued Clemmie became. The good advice given her was wasted.

On the surface Clemmie showed more humour than before. On the inside, a change was taking place.

•••

"It's just such a struggle, Barbara, having to bring da bairns up on my own — I'm nearly a single parent. I see so little o Albert. It's not that they're bad or anything or I wish I hadna had them — I just can't seem to mind a time when things were different, when *I* had some time.

"It's been dis weary routine, year in year out, for as long as I can mind — Albert home for a month or two, and away again. I ken I'm lucky in some ways, I ken there's many a wife would envy me, with the bungalow, and two healthy bairns and a man that's a sea captain. But — it's just so empty.

"I never told you about my sister — I havena told many folk — that's Linda's mother, or she was, poor soul, God rest her. Sometimes I think I'll end up like her, locked away in Kingseat — God forbid — maybe that's why I worry so much about Linda — she's so like her sometimes — poor soul — God rest her — she was always highly strung, but what a lovely lass she was too — I mind — I was a lot younger dan her — I mind when I was a bairn she used to spend her money buying things and hiding them, making up treasure hunts for me and my friends — that's the kind o person she was — lovely, so kind to everybody — but nervous — always highly strung — I suppose I'm like her in dat respect, else I wouldna be here now, ranting on like this. You must think I'm crazy . . .

"It's just — it's been so long since I had anybody I could speak to, I mean like this, about this kind o thing — I almost feel ashamed. But it's because you're an outsider, you see it clearly — I can trust you — can I no?"

•••

The tattered suitcase Albert Henry carried to and from the bungalow at Glimmerwick arrived there in February of 1980 to a colder welcome than on previous occasions. Unlike past home-comings, she did not whisk it away and unpack it eagerly, smiling. It remained on the linoleum floor for hours, opened only for a few seconds when Albert extracted the small gifts he had brought for his wife and children.

Clemmie had something important to say, something that would, in her opinion, change their lives for the better. It had been Barbara Glossop's idea originally.

With the port at Sullom Voe now operational, and tankers calling regularly to fill their bellies with the crude oil stored at the terminal, a fleet of tugs and mooring boats were working out of the harbour, guiding the giant ships through the narrow entrance to Sullom Voe and alongside the jetties. Experienced seamen were employed there, on a shift basis, earning good wages — pilots too.

Albert, with twenty years of experience and a master's ticket, would surely find work there if he applied. Clemmie had the name of a man who would help.

Albert listened silently as she explained. His face was a twisted frown.

"It would be so much better for wis aa, for da bairns, for me, if du was hame more," she said, in conclusion, almost begging with her eyes for his approval.

He slowly shook his head, and sighed loudly.

"Na na, Clemmie."

"What does du mean?"

"It's no use, I couldna spend my working life sailing five miles out and back. I'm a sea captain, no an inshore fisherman, or a bairn in a rowing boat. My dear, du has no idea what du's asking me to do."

She hung over him where he sat in his favourite chair, her face slowly growing angry, while she thought of his selfishness and her trials.

"Be a little more selfish," her friend had said. But Albert would never give her the space for this, he occupied every spare inch himself. She shouted so loudly that the children in the garden heard her.

"Damn de, it's not just for de, it's for aa o wis, me and da bairns too. Selfish! Selfish!"

Now it was his turn to bellow.

"Selfish? And who have I been working for aa dis years if no for you? Christ, Clemmie, du'll better mind dy tongue!"

Clemmie flopped into a chair. There were tears in her eyes.

"She told me. She said it was selfishness."

Albert's anger was tempered by curiosity.

"Who did?" he snapped.

"She told me," she said again, shaking her head, with the tears now issuing freely.

"Who?"

"Damn de, Albert, I'm tired o dis," she sobbed. "Please, just think about it. It's not a silly idea, it could work out best for wis, please."

But Albert's mind was no longer fixed on the tugboats at

Sullom Voe. Clemmie had slipped. Someone had put this thought in her head, someone had been prying into their private lives, Albert knew!

"Who's du been speaking to? What's du been telling folk?"

He got up and crossed the floor to her chair and stood over her threateningly.

"Tell me!" he ordered. Clemmie looked up, shocked and afraid of the aggression in his pose. She hesitated, stopped crying.

"I . . ."

"Tell me," he boomed again.

"It was nothing, Albert. I told her nothing."

His hand moved quickly from its station above her head and caught her solidly on her cheek. She screamed and he, realising what he had done, repented instantly.

"I'm sorry, Clemmie, I didna mean to, I'm sorry . . ."

But the damage was done. The space between them had been breached, by violence. Though they talked quietly and resolved to act as if nothing had happened, though they discussed it all calmly, though Clemmie confessed her secret, it was all too late, for in the act of confiding outside her marriage she had broken not only the seal of the vacuum she had lived in for so long but also the seal of privacy which had surrounded their lives together. And Albert, already ill disposed towards the oil and the incomers, began to regret his notion of making money out of them by renting the cottage. It was a matter of time till he issued the Glossops one month's notice of termination of their lease.

"Soothmoothers," he said, pouring another glass of whisky as he watched them leave. Clemmie stood at the kitchen sink with a sullen look on her face. Since Albert's return, her friendship was over.

Barbara Glossop looked one last time at the little crofthouse she had called her home. Eric, her husband, put his arm around her shoulders and led her to the car. She was confused. but somehow not surprised by this turn of events.

Eric had found another croft, less isolated and with better land, he said. In time she would forget about Glimmerwick, he said. There would be other incomers living near to their new house. They would find it easier to be accepted there.

"Integration," she had said, and had baked a loaf of friendship. But the dough had baked in too hot an oven and was not eaten. Glimmerwick's balance altered once more.

THIN WEALTH

Quhitever rights we tink we hae
Ir sair draan synons ida erm o da laa.
Juist springs o ongyaain kiv
Øsed t'klem life t'døløs ambition.
Athoot a third, maer moderit gait
We tak up black or quhite onkerry,
Fir aa it grey exists, most ordiner
I dis nordren place quhar rain faas
Apo stonn quhile neon gogs
Wi stoory grøt browt be da wind,
Skorpnin opaque, mirk grey nebulae.

Wir intentions, klined laek a pør man's butter,
Thin apo munewatter, wan as munelicht apo an
Øly wattergaa, man owregyaa wir filskit oors
Laek bailiffs raikin trowe an nummerin
Da graet unholy coose o aa wir assets,
Aa cassen awa, juist brukk t'cowp da balance
Owre in favour o da debt dat's aaned wis aa —
Tick black conscience, worn laek a dateless penny,
Packt fir gude luck, atill a secret rivvik,
An yirdit be da face o concrete pørta.

Attenuate
Grow thin
In this lies
A new richness
Mute and wordless.

We spaek lood noo, plaesin uncan fok
Wi guddicks an gab far fae da hert o it
It canna be hid be da hood o cynicism,
Nor yit shested be dis nyaargin t'some
Utadaeks existence — we ging apo most
Antrin amps, skendit be da makkadø o
Sales spaek, inna kirnatansi barter,
Trokin currency o measured tocht
Fir sheeny wanwirts it'll dimmer awa
Tradin glitter fir greyness
Till dir finally forgotten.

We kerry dem t'hirnek hoidies, skaevin oot
Fir da first sign o tak aff, makkin ready
Fir da rim o licht, bit wearin tøtac heads it
Winna ant da ill-faared trowie truths dat
Hing laek dead men fae dir lamp post galloos:
An uncan groth owregyaain moments yit unmade,
Tho da tocht o dem's nipsiccar even noo,
Laek peerie pøshnis berries, likks o da hopless,
Quhaa's intentions ir klined laek a pør man's butter,
Thin apo munewatter, an oil film o da spectrum,
Da vaam an troke o a pør body's wealt wysh.

Attenuate
Grow thin
In this lies
A new richness
Mute and wordless.

Once Linda had made her decision not to go to art college on the mainland, she and Haggerty set about searching for an alternative to life at the fish factory.

She persuaded Mimie a'Wurlie to help her get a job at Firth Camp as a chambermaid, and soon after he found a similar post at Toft Camp nearby. Between them, they were earning nearly £200 a week clear. Finding accommodation was not difficult once they had the money to spend, though the cost of the caravan they rented (in the country in a small scattered village called Nesting, two miles off the main road from Lerwick to Sullom Voe) was far greater than its worth.

They had good times. Lots of parties. Their friends were all in the big money too and there was a heavy scent of euphoria in the air.

It was hard work though: ten hours, seven days a week, plus travelling time there and back. They had made it into the oil boom, but had made sacrifices to get there. They told each other there would be time for art and other things afterwards. There was money to be made meantime.

Before long, euphoria waned and routine set in, like a gangrene, rotting away at the good times.

The caravan became too cramped and they lost interest in keeping it neat and tidy. They both began to drink quite heavily, but not as before in the endless round of parties, now their drinking was done as an escape from the stresses of their lives at Sullom Voe and its dull reality. Money is never earned lightly. Even in the boom time there were heavy costs in terms of personal liberty. It was the time they lost together which was hardest to accept. Their relationship was still young and immature and it needed cultivation. All they had were a few brief hours together at night, then up at six and onto the bus and away.

From time to time, one of them would take a notion for self-discipline and announce, 'I'm going to stop smoking', or some other resolution. But none of their new regimes ever lasted. They were just too tired. Sullom Voe was sucking the energy from them.

They strove to keep a grip on their relationship, to steer it through the difficult stretches. The months passed and they matured quickly. They had to. Their attitudes to work changed. It became something to fight with, a spirited horse to be broken, a cunning adversary in a long drawn-out psychological battle.

But they were saving and told themselves it would be worth while.

Winter was long and dark. The caravan was freezing at night. But worst of all was the wind which used to whip the flimsy structure till it shuddered and shook. Linda would lie awake at night, rigid with fear, waiting for the one big gust which would snap the hawser ties and turn their world over.

As the summer of 1980 approached, the days began to stretch out until they lasted almost till the next dawn, and all the bad feelings of winter slipped away once more. They held beach parties on the shore by the caravan and invited friends from all over. On Midsummer's night they climbed to the top of the hill of Scallafield and watched as the sun dipped low to the horizon then rose again. It rained on the way home, light summer drizzle, but neither cared. They were both high on the experience.

Yet there were few moments of real pleasure. Their lives were speeding out of control and they had too little time to stop and look and absorb things. Next morning the bus was waiting and the continuous round of work went on. As the summer began to fade the all too speedy transition back to winter was upon them. They grew depressed. Their commendable intention to save money had waned. They seemed to need to spend in order to counteract the reality of life at Sullom Voe.

Silently they both went about their business, each thinking the same thing but neither wanting to admit to the other the fact that they had had enough. Enough of the big money, enough of the boom. They were trading their youth for money. . . .

•••

They bought a car to save them walking to catch their bus to work. Haggerty didn't have a licence, but said he could drive, and if they stayed off the main roads they'd be all right. Both applied for driving tests. Although it cost a small fortune to insure the old

Mini they had bought between them, both felt it would be worthwhile.

The first day they had it out, Haggerty reversed it into a dyke and wrecked the rear lights. Linda told him to get out and let her drive, and he started to laugh. She burned his hand with the cigarette she was holding.

"I'm sorry," she said later. "It's that car. It's a bad influence on us. We're getting possessive of it already."

"I wasn't the one who was possessive. *You* told *me* to get out."

"I only meant out of the driver's seat, not the whole car. I thought when you said you could drive, you meant you *could* drive."

"What's that supposed to mean?"

"Nothing, I didn't mean anything, just that you're not as good as I thought you were."

He looked offended and took hold of his burned hand. She bent down and kissed the top of his head.

"Well you're not!"

The car was fun and saved them walking, but it cost a lot of money. It had reached the stage where things were beginning to go wrong regularly. There was always some part in need of renewal. Motor mechanics didn't come easily to Haggerty. His well-intentioned purchases, the spanners and the socket set, remained in their boxes.

At first they stuck to their plan not to use it on the main roads. But time passed and they became bolder about their law breaking. Their friends were scattered all over the islands and the only way to get to visit them was by car. The bus system was almost non-existent. It was handy too for getting to Lerwick for messages and nights out, though Haggerty had become very scathing about Shetland's capital town.

He now believed that much of his dissatisfaction at the fish factory had been a result of living in the town.

"Lerwick?" he would say, "Lerwick is a small town with pretensions of being a capital."

None of their friends disagreed. They looked up to him. They too had moved out of the town to caravans or croft houses, and shared a love of the country. It was a different Shetland from the one which Lerwick seemed to represent. It was beautiful, wild, barren. The coastline was a vast treasure full of natural sculpture. The moorlands were heather wonderlands of peace. Together, in small groups, they walked and smoked hash and talked mystically, picked the magic mushrooms which grew in abundance.

Haggerty's absent days at Toft Camp became more and more frequent, till finally he stopped going altogether. He said he had made all the money he wanted, that he had had all he could take. Linda's puzzlement became annoyance. It had been his idea in the first place, to go there, and save up. Now suddenly he was opting out.

He began to talk again about getting a croft, but she listened without ever taking him seriously, knowing it was a dream. Property was as expensive as ever, and leasing just as difficult. She said nothing, simply listened, aware that he was moving on in his mind. Did she want to go with him, wherever he was headed? She didn't know. She didn't know anything anymore, she was too tired. Somewhere along the line she switched tracks. Someone had changed the points and she was lost. She was no longer a Shetlander. Her speech patterns had changed, her mannerisms, her outlook. Under his promptings, she had joined his little band of wandering friends, of dope-smokers, of drop-outs.

She had taken the key offered her by the spectre in the lane. But it didn't open anything. It was no longer hot and desirable, was instead cold steel from another age whose function was forgotten. She would have to choose her own shape, create her world. Only in smelting would the key be revealed.

Until she knew this secret, she would go on at Sullom Voe, saving money.

•••

Every morning she said hello to her fellow workers in the same half-empty, distanced voice, as if she lived in another dimension, co-existing in their world only passively, without contact. Here lay one of the many puzzles of her life, one of the many small discrepancies which caused her to believe something major was amiss. The false intimacy of her greeting, the tone of voice used. She winced visibly as she spoke.

She knew her world well and her world was incomplete. It was a glass sphere, composed of many thousands of fragments of sharp splinters — angular shapes, sunk and joined in a malleable leaden skeleton.

But at the top, pieces were missing. Wind howled into the interior of her life, rain soaked her pride. There were empty spaces in her stained-glass dome and she knew she had to fill them. But what with?

She collected her keys from the supervisor and went to the corridor she was to clean. The workmen were already on site but they had left their heavy scents behind. Some the brisk smell of aftershave, others the thick musk of body sweat.

When she first began to work there, the older cleaners had mothered her. She was just a peerie Shetland lass to them, and they helped her with the work which she found physically taxing. Linda gritted her teeth and soon she could cope with the job without assistance.

Which was just as well, for it didn't take long for her personal life and the fact that she was living with Haggerty to become common knowledge. The older women changed towards her then. Even Mimie, who she had known nearly all her life.

So her days became solitary, listening to the radio and cleaning. At lunchtimes and break-times she would meet up with some of her younger workmates, but she seemed to have little in common with them, and ate in silence.

She tried to think hard about her future, to make plans. She tried hard to analyse all that had happened to her in the short time since she had left school — the falling out with her family in Glimmerwick, her relationship with Haggerty, her rejection of art college — but somehow her head was never clear enough to really understand the pattern; yet she knew there had to be one.

Time was so packed full of things to do.

She just went along with the flow, rummaging through her days as if they were jumble sale stalls, hunting for a bargain.

While she was out working, Haggerty spent his time lazily. Sometimes he would hitch a lift to Lerwick and go drinking in one of the shorefront bars. Inevitably he would meet a friend and they would soak the day in beer.

Haggerty was expanding his theories on life in Shetland. Once he was full of alcohol, his tongue would loosen the bitterness into bitter words.

"It's the climate," he would say, "it's such a bloody struggle just to keep the heat in and the cold out. No wonder nobody ever has time to do anything creative."

"Nobody makes anything. It's all imported from the mainland, and sold for exorbitant profits called 'freight charges'."

"Lerwick? Lerwick's just a small town with the pretensions of a capital."

The bitterness had filled him. Everyone knew him for it. And they had all heard his opinions before, once too often, even Linda.

Finally, after some months had passed, she working and he drinking, it all burst out like pus from a boil, the festering bitterness. She came home from another day at the camp to find the caravan littered with empty beercans and bottles, with Haggerty sleeping in the middle of it all. He was lying with a cigarette in his hand still burning. She was tired and wanted to go to bed. He woke up and wanted to talk, but it was the same drunken complaints as she had heard too often.

"Parasites, living off people. They don't make anything, they don't *produce*!"

She started clearing the mess from the tiny living space. He lit another cigarette.

"Christ I feel ill!"

"Don't start. I'm tired."

"What the hell do you mean, 'don't start'?" he yelled.

"I've heard it all before, you with a hangover, complaining. You're always running Shetland down, but what I don't understand is what gives you that right?"

He let his face loose into a wide-mouthed grin.

"I keep forgetting. You're a woollyback yourself. I keep forgetting you're a Shetlander!" he laughed.

She restrained herself. Inside she was angry and had suffered these tiny insults so often in silence.

"Maybe you have a dash of Viking blood in you after all. And I thought I'd trained you well . . ."

Haggerty began a furious assault on all things Shetlandic. She tried to ignore him and went to the small kitchen area where she filled the kettle, trying to make space amongst the mess. She knew he was trying to goad her into an argument. But she didn't have the strength to hold it back. She dropped the kettle on the floor where the metal thumped and clashed like a gong. The sound crashed into his conceit, silencing him momentarily.

"Shut up, for Christsake shut up!" she yelled. "You haven't trained me. I'm not your pet. I *am* a Shetlander. So what?"

His quiet persisted only a minute longer. Then the wide grin broke on his face again.

"So I was right was I? You do have a dash of pride left in you?"

She instinctively picked a kitchen knife from the rack of dirty dishes piled above the sink. His face became still more cunning.

"What are you gonna do with that, Linda? Cut me bad?" he sneered.

She stood over him, rigid with a kind of frustration that grew in her heart and spread over her whole body, the saw-edged knife stiff in her grasp. His face hardened till the smile passed away into a look of contempt.

"Put it down before you get hurt," he ordered her.

Suddenly her rigidity relaxed and she swung the knife down quickly, still holding it firm in her grip. Haggerty tried to move out of the way but the sofa springs were old and soft. The knife caught him on the side of the neck, then passed onto the couch where it ripped into the cloth material and the stuffing inside.

Blood began to pour from the wound on his neck.

"Look what you've done," he cried out, fear in voice.

She stood holding the knife for a minute, with her eyes blank and wide. For the first time in her relationship with him, she had taken control.

She could kill him! She could kill him right then, and he was afraid. He knew it. She was his mistress.

She dropped the knife.

•••

"And that's what happened," Linda said quietly. "After I realised what I had done, I took him to the hospital. I left him there. I went to Glimmerwick."

Outside, through the window she could see the sun shining on the sea in Bressay Sound, making it very difficult for her to see the face across the desk from her. The light blinded her, and turned her interviewer into a silhouette.

"And it was your aunt who decided you should come and see me, or did you make that decision yourself?"

She shrugged, then nervously lit a cigarette.

"It was the doctor's idea. But I was willing . . ."

The smoke from her cigarette seemed blue in the sunlight.

"I only asked," the shadowy figure went on, "because unless you are here of your own accord then my job is very difficult. I can only help if the patient allows me."

He moved behind his desk. She nodded. The psychiatrist cleared his throat and opened a thin beige folder lying on the desk in front of him.

"I'd like you to tell me a little about your mother," he said without looking up at her. "Whatever you can remember . . ."

She shrugged, and puffed on her cigarette.

"You don't have to try to tell a complete story. Just whatever you remember . . ." he coaxed.

"I can't remember anything, really."

Again he moved imperceptibly behind the desk. The sun kept flooding through the window.

"You were four when you went to live with your aunt?"

"Yes, only four. I can't remember much before that."

A slow uneasy silence occurred. Linda knew it was for her to break. She sighed and tried to remember something, some starting point. Where did it all begin?

"She was kind," she said finally. It was all she could think to say.

"And she loved plants. I can remember that."

This brought no response from her interrogator. She tried to remember more.

"We lived here in Lerwick. In the lanes above Commercial Street. I don't know where. The house has been knocked down. Where they built the new swimming pool.

"My father was a fisherman. He was lost at sea. Washed overboard."

Still no response. Still he didn't look up from the folder. She tried to remember. All she could see was the sunlight streaming in through the window, blinding her. Then, quite suddenly, she remembered another window, a small kitchen window with a red geranium perched in it, flowering wildly.

"We had a red geranium. She let me water it," she said, half conscious.

"It used to grow . . ." She hesitated. "My mother, she had a red geranium in the kitchen window. Its petals were red, blood red."

She took another draw from her cigarette. She was beginning to recall pictures that had been behind locked doors.

A shutter in her mind was beginning to lift.

"And there was a man. I used to be frightened of him. He used to walk past our house."

"And you were frightened by him? Why?"

"It was at night. Every night."

She could hear the slip-slap of his footsteps on the stone steps outside. . . .

"It was silly, really. He was a baker. We used to live behind the bakery. He was only on his way to work."

She stubbed out the half-smoked cigarette and licked her mouth inside. She hated the taste after smoking.

Inside, the doors kept opening, in chorus-line synchronicity.

"I suppose all kids are scared of something. He was my bogey-man. I remember one time he looked up at my bedroom window when I was looking out. I got such a fright."

She gave a short nervy laugh.

"Silly, really. I suppose all kids are scared of something."

The shadowy figure moved again behind the desk. Through

the red aura of the sun she could just make out the faint outline of a soft beard and spectacles.

"How did you feel when your father died?"

The question came at her out of the red mist.

"I ... I ..."

A long silence.

"I mind the rain, and the wind, and my mother crying. That's all."

"And when your mother went away, what then?"

"I ..."

Another long silence, which bore nothing.

"When you went to live with your aunt and uncle, were you afraid of them?"

"No," she answered, quite firmly. "Clemmie was good to me. And Albert too, sometimes."

"Not all the time?"

Linda laughed again, another short nervy exhalation.

"Sometimes he would make me greet. He could be cruel and make me greet."

She was reverting back to her natural tongue, slowly. The intonation of her speech patterns was changing back.

"What did he do to make you cry?"

"He would tell me that I wasn't their bairn."

"And did you want to be?"

"No ... I just wanted Mammy."

"When did he tell you that you weren't his child?"

"If I called him 'Dad' or Clemmie 'Mammy'."

She lit another cigarette.

"He'd get mad and tell me I wasn't his bairn ..."

She took a long draw of the blue smoke. Her eyes had ceased to try to see. They had pulled down a thin blind of skin to prevent the bright light from hurting.

"And did this upset you?"

"Ja. It did. I'd go off on my own somewhere and make plans."

"What kind of plans?"

A smile spread across her face, a smile of childish guile.

"Plans how I'd go away and get money and come back and then they'd want me."

"And did that make you feel better?"

Her smile vanished into a frown, still childish but troubled.

"Ja, I'll make dem sorry . . ."

She seemed to drift into a space of her own then. The thought of her childish plans of vengeance pleased her. She smiled again, that same smile of naive cunning.

The soft warm voice came out of the red . . .

"Did they tell you where your mother was?"

"Sometimes. Clemmie said she was ill. But Albert told her to tell the truth."

"And did she?"

Suddenly she seemed to snap out of her vacancy, and her dark moonish eyes became sharply focused. The bright lights blinding her dimmed and the room grew dark. She saw the man's face across the desk from her, and hesitated on the brink of speech. Was he a stranger? Could he be trusted with the secret? The sunlight swelled again and her mind became blood-red.

"Did she tell you the truth?"

She trembled. A small bead of crystal water appeared in the corner of her eye.

"She's dead," she cried out. "Dead for years. Dey tried to keep it a secret. She killed hersel."

Tears lubricated dry eyes, bright reds faded into duller colours. Linda opened the shutter in her mind fully, till the light streamed in and washed away her hurt, till she finally admitted to her inner self the truth she had heard all those years before and had since repressed. Inside, she felt release oozing over her, easing her mind, a soft natural opiate which cooled her fever. The figure of the man in the Lerwick lane lost his shadows and stood in a shaft of red sunlight with nothing hidden from her. He had a wide face, with eyes set apart in his head, joined by a flat, yet faintly curved sheet of bone forehead.

He had a wide mouth. And there on his neck was a long angular scar, half-healed, and blood pouring from its other half.

She shivered. Her mind instantaneously sharp and alert. She looked through the window out to the sea, and the cliffs of Bressay.

The sun had been covered by a blank of grey cloud. The water no longer shimmered.

•••

Haggerty was on his way home. The *St. Clair* steamer ploughed southwards, away from Shetland and the distant outline of its southernmost tip at Sumburgh Head.

He was standing on the deck, watching the trail of angry water as it churned in violent green spins in the wash, tailing off behind the ship.

He had had his adventure after all. The scar on his neck was almost healed now. He was proud of it in a perverse way. It was a sort of proof of his manhood.

And he had made her do it. He took full responsibility. He knew it. He had forced her to strike out and hurt when his threat pushed too close, as Shetland would strike out at oil if pushed too far.

He looked back to Sumburgh Head, and laughed. It was a proper exchange. He had given her a kind of wealth by stripping away her preconceived notions of how life ought to be led. And she had made him a man, had brought the first real drama to his life.

It was a fair exchange. Out of it something good had happened. He had written a poem. Not that he had never written poetry prior to this. He had often, but it had never been *his* work before, free of the influence of other writers he had read.

He was not at liberty, but always free.

•••

Linda spent two months in Glimmerwick, living quietly with her aunt and uncle. They were surprised at her sudden return, but took her in immediately when they saw how distressed she was. She never did explain what had happened. And they in return never pushed her. They gave her space when she most needed it and a new closeness resulted. She never once said 'I was wrong' — and didn't necessarily believe she had been, but she respected their well-intended lectures, and loved the attention they gave her.

Soon, the time came when she knew she had to leave. Clemmie and Albert seemed to know as well. They let her go, with good wishes, wherever she was headed.

Linda was going back into the Sullom Voe vortex. It had left her breathless and breaking surface tensions. She wanted to conquer it, and do what she had started out to do.

To save money.

They let her go.

•••

Glimmerwick had lain quiet for some time following the departure of the Glossops for their new croft. Mimie continued her tiresome round of work and sleep at Firth Camp, still saving hard. Lowrie wandered about the croft like a lost dog. He seemed to have grown much older of late. The stoop in his back had become much more pronounced.

Clemmie retreated back inside her bungalow shell. The children were happy enough, still just as much of a handful. Albert was at sea, on a tanker en route to the Middle East with a cargo from Sullom Voe, of all places. His career was taking him quite close to home now and again.

As time went by, life in Glimmerwick settled into a kind of pattern once again. The pattern was the intermediate between the beginning and the end of end of oil, a thin oily sheen on the waters of their lives. It was an affluent pattern. Lowrie was considering replacing his old Bedford van with a Japanese model, and Albert parked a new car at his doorstep. The fields in Glimmerwick seemed greener again. Whatever traumas had surrounded the coming of oil were now happily resolved, even if the scars remained.

The balance of the place had been changed so often in so short a space of time that no one really knew what the balance was. These new values which weighed the sides of that balance were not right, not wrong. It wasn't a choking of native tradition, but

129

E

simply change. What was wrong was the speed of that change. It was utterly manufactured and unnatural. And Lowrie, whilst aware of the benefits, refused to admit that the oil era had been a successful one for his home. He knew that this pattern was only a temporary stop in the greater flux, and that it would be sharply destroyed once the money stopped flowing. He knew, and remained passive, watching. It was out of his hands. He simply sat by the stove side, nodding his head, and telling himself that he had been right all along. He was absorbing the time of oil into the library of Shetland's folklore which he stored in his old grey head. It was already a part of history.

And of his story. . . .

And then the news leaked out that someone had bought the half-finished Haa of Glimmerwick. The grapevine had it that the new owner was the manager of Sullom Voe Terminal. This rumour persisted for a couple of weeks, and had an odd effect on the people living there. They didn't know whether they should feel flattered or threatened.

The builders who had left so abruptly years before, when Stokowski had disappeared, then returned. They worked quickly, being left to the job this time, instead of constantly interrupted by their employer. Within a few months, the old Haa was completed. Whoever the mysterious new owners were, they had spared no money on refurbishing it.

When the full story emerged, it turned out that it was one of the management team at Sullom Voe who had bought the house, although not the ultimate chief as was rumoured. The man in question was a petroleum engineer from London, important enough. He was married, but had no children. The couple were in their late thirties. Both worked at Sullom Voe.

They, Mr and Mrs Butler, moved into their new home with very little fuss. It was some time before they were even seen by their neighbours. In the mornings, their car was gone and did not arrive back in Glimmerwick till darkness had fallen. Mimie said she thought they still had a company house in Brae and hadn't moved in properly yet.

And this was how things continued. In time, Lowrie and Mimie and Clemmie and the children grew used to seeing the Butlers' car, and their faces, but few words were exchanged. They made it plain from the beginning that they had no desire to mix. And unlike the Glossops before them, the Butlers had little interest in the land, or the beauty of the place. Their lives were spent in the interior of the Haa house, even more distant from the common folk of Glimmerwick than the old lairds of pre-war times.

Inside the Haa, Joan and Oliver Butler enjoyed every comfort. They had installed a large Aga stove and central heating. They did not use peat, but instead had coal delivered all the way from Lerwick. Their lives revolved around the oil terminal. After all, that was the real reason for their being there. The Haa house was simply an investment.

As far as Lowrie was concerned, they neither contributed to nor asked for anything from Glimmerwick. But in a way, the fact that they were there, the fact that the Haa was occupied comforted him. It reminded him of the old days. He was glad to see the old house full of lights at night. It had been a shell for far too long.

Their coming did not upset the intermediate pattern of life, only thickened the thin oily sheen on the waters, by swelling the mood of affluence in the settlement.

Neither did it in any way alter the future predicted by the old crofter. When the money ceased flowing, the Butlers would go. And it might be sooner than anyone believed.

•••

Oliver Butler put on his round yellow safety hat and left the comfort of his office at Sullom Voe Terminal. The sky was clear above, except for the plume of smoke rising into the blue from the vicious flames shooting out the main gas flare at the top of the hill.

He walked slowly along the edge of the tarmac roads on site, his portly stomach sticking out in front, his hands clasped behind his back. He was on a tour of inspection, having little else to do. Land Rovers and vans roared past him, busily moving plant and hands around the expansive site to the places they were needed.

Oliver climbed the hill behind the main office block, till he stood in a position of far seeing. He scanned the panorama slowly. Of the four jetties which stuck out into the deep of the voe, three were in use; the fourth would soon become functional too, handling liquid petroleum gases instead of crude oil as the others did.

Inland, giant pipes sprawled and intertwined — huge metal vessels roared below him, in the process plant where the volatile crude oil entering the terminal was pacified by means of computerised control of pressure and temperature, which allowed the high-pressure gas to flash off into special containers. Distillation columns poked above the complex. Everything worked simultaneously, as the workforce came and went, one shift relieving the other.

Oliver recalled the first time he had seen the site, back in 1976, before he had actually moved north to take up his present position. Then it was simply a muddy hillside. Now the terminal was more or less complete. Certainly there was still work to be done, but the end was quite clearly in sight.

The Shetlands. He had never even heard of them prior to the oil strikes. He had had no idea of their location. Yet here he was, with his life inextricably braided in with that of these islands.

But extricate himself he would, in time, when he felt he was ready. Joan would follow. She was a top-class secretary and would find work wherever his career took him.

•••

During 1981, talk of redundancies at the oil terminal began to consume the workers' minds. The construction phase was almost complete and the official opening was scheduled for the 8th of May, when H.R.H. the Queen, Elizabeth II, and her entourage would bless the venture.

For the catering staff, the end was delayed until the following year. Voluntary pay-offs trimmed the workforce away till the coming of Christmas brought the camps' closure. Mimie a'Wurlie was one of the smiling women who collected their final cheque from the wages office at Firth Camp — poor red-faced Mimie, who had been the subject of so much worry with her panting and peching. But she stuck it out and now her bank balance stood at a remarkably high figure for an 'aald croftin wife'. Canada beckoned.

For Linda, the end was a less pleasant affair. Since Haggerty's departure, she had lived a solitary life in her caravan and at the camp, mixing with only one or two good friends, reading and learning to paint all over again. She did not visit the township at Glimmerwick. All that seemed so far away — the bungalow, Clemmie and Albert and their children, Lowrie and Mimie. But she often dreamt of the place itself and of the secret places she had visited as a child. Her life had settled into a routine of a kind, which although trying was satisfying in a way too. She was saving money and so preparing for the next stage of her life. She tried to look ahead.

But when the moment came to let go of the boom and the big money, she could not break away. Instead she got involved in a drinking session in one of the blocks, something she had never done since the very early days when she and Haggerty had partied all the time. Some of the last remaining catering staff were having themselves a farewell to Shetland which they would remember. They too were finding it difficult to leave — some had given up much to work there — wives and families. Linda joined them and in half an hour was roaring drunk on whisky and coke.

Her head was spinning. She laughed at everything. So did everyone. It was remarkable! If she laughed, so did they! What a power to have over people! But after a short time she began to feel sick and dizzy and then the room was spinning too. Suddenly everything was horrible and dark. The faces no longer laughed, they snarled. Each one wore a mask. They were wolves and she had always been a lamb. They were tearing away her flesh with their teeth. But her flesh was money. Every bite they took was nothing but torn twenty pound notes!

She woke with a sudden relief. A faint morning light filtered through drawn curtains. She had little recollection of what had happened. But she recognised the curtains.

She sat upright in the bed; the curtains were the same gaudy pattern which hung in every room in the camp — and she was naked. Beside her lay a naked man — old and wrinkled and snoring loudly. She half recognised him too — it was the kitchen porter who kept offering her hunks of steak to take home. The thought of this meat and the blood running out of it, the smell of stale food lingering on his clothes made her feel sick again. The taste of her vomit persisted in her mouth. She leapt from the small single bed to the sink, where she spewed — her stomach was empty and nothing emerged. She simply retched over the empty bowl seven times as the taps ran in a rush, splashing water on her face. Each surge of muscular contraction twisted her face with strain.

She sat on the floor, her head reeling, then slowly rose up and took her crumpled, dirty clothes from beside the bed. She could feel the night before come seeping out her pores, and the smell of food seemed to have been rubbed into every crevice. She was sick. Sick of Sullom Voe, of men, of everything. Of Shetland and of people.

Half crying in self-pity, half shouting at herself for her stupidity, she left the camp for the last time.

She walked the quarter mile down to the main road and waited in the drizzle, trying to thumb a lift. She thought how not so long ago, the roads around here were as busy as city streets. Now the fleets of buses were gone. She looked around the voe of Firth at the scattering of crofthouses swamped by estates of homogeneous concrete. Somewhere in the heart of it all lay an older Shetland which she had not yet seen. Then a car appeared, headed towards Lerwick, and she waved her hand at it, thumb prominent in a clenched fist. The driver seemed happy enough not to talk. She was relieved and half shut her eyes. The cassette player was buzzing, producing the pained tones of Tammy Wynette singing a mournful country ballad about rejection.

When she finally reached her caravan, she turned the key in the lock but found the door was stuck, swollen with dampness. She had to exert all her strength to force it open. Inside, everything was cold and damp. She opened the curtains and put the kettle on to boil. Outside she saw the winter wind blow the wizened grass into waves and sweep the sheltered waters with an icy blast. Her mood filled with sadness. She felt dirty. How had all this happened to her? She was twenty-three, with thousands of pounds in the bank, and she was feeling as if the world was ending.

Where had it all begun? Was there any point which marked its origins, this pathway of hers, or had it always been happening? Even before she was born? How would it appear if it were written down, the legend, the myth of her life? Ordinary as it might seem to those who did not live it, to Linda it was a torture. What formed its flesh? The steamy sensual experiences or the cold mouldings of time and distance, her own inimitable education in the gaps that lie between people and the vacuum of solitary existence?

When it grew dark, which it did quite early that grey day, she lit a candle. She had no change for the meter left. She wrapped blankets around her and sat smoking cigarettes till dawn, listening to the all-night radio from London. At least she still had batteries in the transistor.

The transistor! Clemmie had sent her a message, inviting her to come to Glimmerwick for the New Year. Linda felt at once warm and alone. As the hours passed, she thought about Glimmerwick and her life there. She still felt so much for the place. No matter where else she lived, she could never feel at home. Glimmerwick was so unique. It had no substitute. Yet it had never been her true home. She was an orphan — God how she hated the word — and all her time with Clemmie had been no more than charity. Now she was an adult, she was expected to look after herself. Clemmie had told her as much, when they had argued over Haggerty. But she still missed the place — more so than her own parents even.

Linda washed in freezing cold water till her body felt clean and fresh. She switched everything off and locked the caravan door behind her. She coaxed her Mini till the engine started.

She drove south to Lerwick and parked on Victoria Pier. Flat calm water reflected back zigzagged images of the old town, a distinctive horizon of familiar buildings which had been fitted together over the years. But the little house behind the bakery was long gone. The place where it had stood was now part of the new swimming pool and car park.

Linda gazed out over the tide to the island of Bressay, where the televison mast stood erect in the mists, and was suddenly aware of her story.

Part Three: Pale New Mune

On the basis of the estimated size of, and production schedules for, currently proven fields alone, the peak of Shetland's oil period may be past within ten years. It seems that known reserves will be fully exploited by 1985 . . . that the largest fields have been discovered already.

From *The Shetland Report: A Constitutional Study.*

Prepared for the Shetland Islands Council
by the Nevis Institute, Edinburgh,
published 1978.

AFTER THE BALL IS OVER

January the 31st, 1983, was one of those all too rarely perfect days in Shetland, when the sun moves through the blue sky uninterrupted and the sea lies passive at the shore. Then, all the sleeping colours awake, and the land glows with a million hues of brown and gold.

It was a day to remember, the first remarkable day of good weather that year. Then, as ever, the cost of that day's pleasure arrived, blowing in on the north wind. The snow began. And it went on, and on, and on.

By morning the road past the voehead at Glimmerwick had blocked. The Butlers couldn't get to work. They waited for the snowplough, but it never came. The road to Glimmerwick was well out of the way and one of the last concerns for the gang of roadmen responsible for its clearance.

At night, the electricity supply failed. Lowrie fetched the old Tilley lamp, filled it with oil, trimmed its wick, and soon Mimie could see to go on with her knitting. Clemmie's window also lit up with the yellow glow.

In the Butlers' Haa, Oliver struck matches and cursed as they burned his fingers, while Joan rummaged in a cupboard, searching for the portable gas lamp they'd used on camping trips to the continent.

"Aha," she cried, the sound of rattling crockery punctuating her fumbling, and pulled out, not the lamp, but a rather gaudy vase an aunt had sent her for Christmas. Another match faded and dulled.

"Well, that was the last one," Oliver informed her.

"There's another box in my handbag," she replied.

"And where's your handbag?"

"In the car."

"The car," he groaned, "I'm not going out there. You'll find me in the morning like some prehistoric mammoth frozen in a glacier, still rummaging through your handbag."

"Well get a light from the Aga then," she said sharply.

"What with?"

"Use your initiative, Ollie!"

And so they continued, until Joan remembered the ornamental candles in their bedroom.

•••

The snow lay for a week. Clemmie waited anxiously for it to clear. Albert had four months leave due to him, and he was due home that week. He was taking time off to help Lowrie with the voar work on the crofts.

Clemmie busied herself, giving the bungalow a good spring-cleaning. She wanted to get everything shipshape before he arrived.

He'd bring them presents. He always did. Not anything extravagant but curios from the edges of the world, that sort of thing. Silks and perfumes for her, trinkets for the bairns.

He'd come in, and set his old battered suitcase on the kitchen floor by the chair he hadn't filled for months. He'd silently light his pipe, while Clemmie and the bairns waited eagerly for his words.

The aromatic smoke from his tobacco would fill the air, greeting the smell of the peat fire — old friends reunited. His beard, impregnated with the smell of the tobacco, would shake as he began to speak. He had a gruff voice, her Albert, which seemed to lose its clarity as it passed through the filter of his moustache. . . .

Clemmie started. Daydreaming again, and so much to do. . . .

•••

Albert's return was delayed. He telephoned from Glasgow.

"Hello, Clemmie?"

"Yes, where is du?"

"Glasgow. I'm stranded here. Are you aa well?"

"Yes. When'll du be home?"

"I'll get da first plane I can."

It was a bare conversation and didn't satisfy Clemmie.

She set the receiver back on its perch and breathed a cloud of moist air into the chilled hallway. It was a cold afternoon.

Then the wind rose from the south, and by morning the thaw was complete. The children groaned and wouldn't eat their porridge, but the Sullom Voe commuters were pleased. Lowrie too welcomed the thaw. There was work to be done, a score of little handyman jobs of the type he loved doing.

•••

Albert arrived the following day.

"Tangier, Bangkok and Singapore," he growled, distributing his gifts. The children oohed and aahed as they unwrapped their parcels. Clemmie murmured thanks as he handed her a bolt of gaily coloured silk.

"Du'll make desel a dress for da regatta dance. Du'll have time, will du no?" he said, not expecting a reply.

Clemmie ran her fingers over the material.

"Yes," she smiled, "but it's awful thin and . . ."

"Then line it, dear Clemmie," he sang, in the manner of the old song. She said no more. There was no point in arguing. He sucked on his pipe, sending billows of smoke upwards. She looked him over, sitting there in his old favourite chair. He was ageing now, becoming coarse, ruddy red cheeks, grey through his beard.

He turned his attention to the bairns.

"And do you like what I've brought you?" he asked them.

For Isaac, a clay pipe, its bowl in the mould of an Arab's head. For Ellen, a doll in the Thai national costume. And a third shared gift, a carved wooden monkey strung between two sticks, which somersaulted acrobatically when the string was pulled tight. They clamoured their thanks, eyes bright with delight.

"And how's da boat?" he boomed to Isaac.

"High and dry," the little boy cried, recognising a family rejoinder.

"Dan we'll get her low and wet," came the traditional punchline, and the family laughed, as they always did, at every homecoming.

Clemmie herded the children outside.

"Take care o dem noo," she warned, pointing to their presents. "Dey've come a lang way to be yours."

The clatter of feet subsided. Albert rubbed his beard.

"Aye but it's good to be home," he said stretching.

"An du has four whole months wi wis?"

"Aye, four whole months."

"I wish it wis four whole years," Clemmie sighed. "Du has no idea what it's like here without de."

Albert's booming voice became suddenly kind.

"Now Clemmie, we've been aa through dis. I'm a seaman, a damned good wan. I could never settle to anything else."

He got up from his chair and placed his smouldering pipe on the table carefully. He knew what was coming, he knew what she would say next. As if to intercept the words, he moved across to where she sat, her chin resting on her hands, her slim forearms supporting the weight of her worry as she leant forward with her elbows on the old table. He looked at her until she blushed, till she began fiddling with the strands of hair that were hanging down over her face.

"I'm in an awful state for dy first day home. Look at dis grey hair. Du most think me ugly."

She spoke, not seeking compliments, but with a note of apology in her plaintive voice.

"Silver," he said, "pure silver. A beautiful woman never grows old."

Clemmie smiled, a little embarrassed by this flattery.

"Wance upon a time, du'd have called me a lass," she whispered, avoiding his stare. He walked over to her, bent down till his face was so close that his smell, his own inimitable smell, caught hold of her sense, sent her swooning in a giddy remembering.

"Wyrds! Dat's only wyrds," he breathed, the pungent smell of his tobacco on his tongue. "Du's still lovely. Will du no give me a kiss, noo dat I'm finally here in da flesh?"

She turned her head and looked up at him, searching for some sign of understanding. Her eyes were tired and sad, her lips dolefully down-turned.

"Bide hame," she whispered. "Give it up. Du could get a job at Sullom Voe, on wan o da pilot boats."

He said nothing. He bent and picked her up, deftly, from the table where she leant, her small thin-limbed body like a child's in his arms. She made no protest. This was tradition too, this lovemaking on his return. He carried her down the hallway to their bedroom, pushed open the door with his foot, and laid her gently on the bed, not once looking her full in the face.

His expression remained stiff and blank, half his face lost in the dark beard. As she watched him undress, with his back to her, she wondered how it had come to this between them, this silence, this muteness, this wall of resistance.

"Albert," she said softly, "give it up. Bide hame."

He stopped the unknotting of his tie, turned, and sat down on the bed. He stared at her with that expressionless face she knew so well, a blankness which hid his desire for her. He placed a large rough hand on her breast. She felt a confusion of emotions inside her, fighting for supremacy. She wanted his powerful masculinity, but she wanted more than that alone. He continued to ignore her pleas. She was imprisoned inside her comfortable home, only able to reach out through the bars and touch him on his terms, through physical unity.

He lay down on the bed beside her. She felt the mattress sink below his heavy body. He began kissing her neck. She smelled his scent full in her throat. She submitted. She opened herself to him, and he pushed inside her like the bull he was.

•••

Afterwards, he assumed his other self again, rising from her side

144

immediately, talking to her idly, shoving the pleasure they had shared behind him.

"Dey'll be a lot o voar wark to be done," he mumbled, fixing his tie. Clemmie bit her lip, but couldn't repress the sob. Albert looked troubled, then turned away from her, and, sighing, left the room.

He walked down the hall. In the kitchen, he heard the children talking quietly. He went outside, found himself plunged into a winter's night. The remaining hollows of the snow crumped and croaked beneath his boot soles.

He wondered at Clemmie and her ways. She seemed a stranger, shy and secretive. That coy humour she had shown to him when they were courting had gone, like the girl in her. Time had brought out the hidden things about her, till she turned clear inside out and the parts he had loved were locked away, out of reach.

Still, he knew they remained and this increased his frustration. He knew that their lovemaking was an empty ritual, an action done for no good reason. He knew that it hurt her, not in the physical sense, but in a worse fashion, and in some perverse way he relished that knowledge.

But when the act was complete, it was he that felt the pain and the guilt, and she was triumphant over him, martyred in her own bed.

He knew her torture, but couldn't spare her. It wasn't his hand that turned the screw on the rack. The culprit was the ocean, like some huge mystic magnet, drawing him from her, a force he couldn't resist. Her rival, the ocean.

The stars glinted in the clear sky, quite close at hand, almost within reach. He stopped by the peatstack at the corner of the house, and looked up, inspecting their display. They were present on land as they were at sea, and he loved them. He could navigate by the stars, could find his way across dark water without mead or map. If only life ashore were as simple.

A breeze blew softly, in from the open sea. Albert felt it on his cheek, and knew it as a friend. For a moment, he thought he heard a voice, calling to him through the mirk. He craned his neck, but the sound did not recur. Puzzled, he retraced his steps, and went back into the tension of the bungalow.

He'd only been back a few hours. Yet already she was eating away at his peace of mind. He wasn't an unfeeling man. He *knew* her torture. But he couldn't spare her.

And so the gulf of the unspoken separated them, and that gulf filled with guilt.

•••

Below the township of Glimmerwick, on the slope down to the shore, the cultivated fields lay dormant, corn rigs bristling with withered stubble, tattie rigs bare. Lowrie watched as Albert positioned the tractor and plough to begin another year of growth. Like a partner in a dance, the machine seemed to halt and bow, addressing the corner of the field.

The angle of the plough dug into the soil as the tractor jolted forward, clutch slipping, then as the smooth forward motion began, the fresh umber earth turned aside from the blade as the plough scythed through the dead skin of winter. Even from his vantage point, Lowrie could hear the soft swish of the blade as it opened the land to cultivation, a welcome sound that he loved, occasionally broken by a metallic ring as stones caught the steel.

Lowrie recalled the old Iron Horse he had ploughed with before the tractor came, an engine on wheels with two great handles. He recalled it with nostalgic regret at its passing, though at the time it had ached his arms till they were nearly pulled out of their sockets.

He was sitting atop a ladder which was perched up against the byre roof. He held an old tarbrush and a pot of black tar stood on the gentle incline of the gable wall. The roof had been leaking. He set down the tarbrush on the roof so that it wouldn't slide off, then fumbled in his pocket for the half-smoked roll-up he had placed there earlier. His backside just about fitted onto the top rung of the ladder, so there he sat. He looked about him at the spring which had come too soon, and watched as the tractor and plough moved through the first furrow of 1983.

Out of some long-shut closet, a picture of his grandfather and the team of horses he had used came into his head. For a while, it was vivid: the long grey beard, the cap he had worn (a cheesecutter), the steamy breath of the horses as they came under harness willingly and tamely. Powerful equine limbs stomping through the matted rig, under command as surely as the accelerator pedal on the tractor they now used.

Lowrie had ploughed with a team as a boy, though never in earnest. It had made a deep impression on him, of wild power at his fingertips that at any time might break loose. Suddenly the faces of the old people he had known when he was young filled his head, long-dead residents of Glimmerwick who were surely rotted away into the soil of the graveyard. He remembered how they had rejected so many of the innovations technology had brought them, preferring instead to perservere with the old hard ways they knew and trusted. He'd thought them foolish, obstinately stuck in the past.

They'd laughed at him when he brought his first motor bike home, an old BSA, had laughed at the way he sat gingerly astride it, while the engine roared and coughed simultaenously between his legs.

"Yon'll take a coarn o taming, Lowrie lad."

"Keep da bit firm in its teeth, mind!"

And now he was as they had been, crossed by the unpredictable path of change. Changing methods, changing values. He laughed at the thought without bitterness.

Maas like hungry beggars at the heels of a rich man dived and swooped behind the plough in a nebulous cloud of white wings and ringing cries. Fat and juicy worms found their subterranean safety overturned, were exposed to daylight, then gulped into another darkness where the digestive fluids of their predators began the taking of their simple lives.

It was a cycle which seemed to have no end: voar, summer, hairst and winter, on and on. Yet every season was different. Nothing was ever really the same. Time always left its mark, its scar.

The tractor began its slow trundle once more, and the cloud of birds reassembled behind it. Lowrie threw the cigarette end from his hand and as he did so his sleeve caught the handle of the tarbrush, sending it sliding down the roof. He made a grab for it, but only succeeded in speeding its descent. He wobbled for a moment at the top of the ladder, then overbalanced and fell backwards.

For an instant he saw the stone beneath him, a breath away, then knew no more as his grey head hit the cold hard surface of the briggistanes.

At ten-past one, Mimie gave up waiting. It wasn't like Lowrie to be late when there was food around. She went out and called on him. There was no reply. She walked out till she could see the tractor below, still ploughing, but there was no sign of Lowrie. She went to the byre where he had been tarring and there she found him lying on the stone path, his head split open, the ladder over his crumpled body. He was unconscious.

In a blind panic, she ran down over the fields calling out to Albert. He didn't hear her above the noise of the tractor. She was almost down at his side before he happened to look up and see her. She blurted out what had happened. Albert went running. He carried Lowrie into the house. Mimie came panting after him, red-faced.

"I telld him he was too old for climbing ladders," she said breathlessly. "I telld him."

Albert laid him out on the ben-room settee. He took charge of the situation and ordered Mimie to go out and get Clemmie, and phone the doctor. Mimie seemed glad of direction and rushed off to the bungalow.

The doctor came as quickly as he could. He examined Lowrie and telephoned the hospital. An ambulance was sent out.

Clemmie made pot after pot of tea, trying to calm Mimie's nerves. She took a cup through to the doctor in the ben-room.

"Is it serious?" she asked in a whisper.

The doctor, a large man in country clothes which made him look more like a fisherman than a physician, shrugged.

"Can't say. It'll depend on the X-rays. Apart from the obvious injury to his head, he seems to have fallen on something which caught him on his spine."

He took the cup of tea from Clemmie. "I've given him a sedative for the present till the ambulance gets here," he informed.

Clemmie stood staring at the figure lying on the sofa.

The doctor eyed her carefully.

"Any more trouble with your nerves?" he enquired.

She started, shook her head.

"No no," she answered, "Albert, my man, is home just now. It makes an awful difference."

And at that moment, Clemmie's worries were far from her mind. When she'd visited the doctor in his surgery at the end of the previous year, she'd been in a bad way, with her nerves tight like fiddle-strings. But there was nothing he could really do for her, other than prescribe tranquillisers. It was cases like hers that made him wish he *was* a fisherman.

•••

The ambulance stopped outside the hospital in Lerwick. Lowrie felt himself lifted and carried inside on a stretcher. The blinding pain and the drugs prevented the full functions of his senses. Still he was peculiarly aware of where he was. Sixty-three and he'd never been in hospital in his life, until now.

Faces peered down at him where he lay, defenceless like a dog exposing its throat to its enemy in submission. Agony flooded through him from some unknown point. Voices muttered out of earshot. Pungent scents of disinfectant and sterile cleanliness toyed with his nostrils. He fell into a furious sleep through which he was pursued by the pain in a maze of cornstooks and peatstacks. 'X-rays', he heard through the mists. A nurse stuck a huge face in front of his and spoke words in a loud clear voice but he couldn't put the sounds together into meaning. He saw a hypodermic needle being primed, saw it being pointed at him, felt the pin stick in his skin. The anaesthetic swept through his system in a few seconds that seemed like eternity.

•••

Clemmie and Mimie waited anxiously. A nurse brought them some tea. Clemmie suggested they should go home as there was nothing they could do there but wait, but Mimie shook her head.

"I'll no go till I hear something," she said firmly.

They watched the clock chase round the hours. Darkness fell, staff came and went. At last, they were admitted to the ward where Lowrie had been sent. A nurse took them to his bed. There he lay, still under the influence of the anaesthetic, his head now carefully bandaged in a turban-like swathe. The bedclothes were hoisted from his body by some kind of cage under the covers. Mimie stared at him lying there, surrounded by all the medical paraphernalia and turned away from Clemmie to hide her expression.

The ward was small and overcrowded. The overspill from the inadequately small old folk's home were squeezed into the casualty ward. In the beds to either side of Lowrie were two old men, one thin and gaunt who played endless games of patience with bony hands, and one who simply lay staring at the blank ward walls with a solemn solitary face. Periodically he sat bolt upright, as if about to call out, then would lie back on the bed again, and resume his former vacancy.

The implications of Lowrie's fall bullied their way to Mimie's thoughts.

"He'll never be back in Glimmerwick more," she breathed.

Clemmie understood, and softly laid her hand on Mimie's shoulder.

"Du'll see," she whispered, "he's a tough auld fellow is our Lowrie."

Yet she too felt something strangely disturbing about this place, these old folk uprooted at the dusk of their lives and taken from the places they have lived in and loved, brought here to this empty existence to be kept alive by modern medicine and constant vigilance. What kind of life was it for these poor old folk? Life at all costs, without regard for the kind of life. Life measured not in the currency of enjoyment but the false perception of time.

Clemmie knew what Mimie meant.

In the car on the way home, Mimie was silent, thinking over

what the doctor at the hospital had told her. Clemmie switched on the radio quietly to ease the tension.

Finally Mimie spoke.

"I'd rather he'd been killed than made to live in a home," she said with a tear." "God spare me for saying it, but it's true."

Inside herself, Clemmie agreed. But for Mimie's benefit she smiled and spoke kindly.

"Du'll see, he'll be well in no time."

"He might be," Mimie said without conviction. "I'll need to phone da boys in Canada."

Clemmie glanced at her. "I could do it if du wanted . . ." she offered.

"No," said Mimie, "it's all right, I'll manage."

Broken bones heal slowly in old people, if they heal at all. With his skull fractured and two vertebrae cracked, Mimie was preparing herself for the worst. Although he'd always been a healthy robust man, he was by no means young anymore.

A vision of how it would be at Wurlie without him came into her mind. The lonely nights, the single plate on the table, the unread copy of the *Scottish Farmer*, all the little adjustments she would have to make to her life. To *their* life, the life they had forged together over the years till its routines and responsibilities were perfectly understood by both of them and they existed side by side filling the middle ground without overlap, confident of each other's movements like dancing partners neatly avoiding each other's toes. Even her time at Sullom Voe hadn't upset things. But this!

•••

Albert poured himself another glass of whisky. He lit his pipe. Clemmie still wasn't back from the hospital. Agitated, he paced the room. Perhaps he should have gone instead. It was a long drive to Lerwick.

He couldn't help thinking on the implications of Lowrie's fall. If his injuries were as serious as it seemed, then Clemmie's pleas for him to leave the sailing would carry all the more weight.

There would be a responsibility to stay at home and run the crofts, and Albert could not easily decline a responsibility.

The lights of a car flashed in the window. He looked out. It was them. He waited as the car stopped, doors shut, and they entered the bungalow.

Clemmie turned to Albert with an air of authority.

"Make a cup of tea for Mimie, would du?"

Her tone so surprised him that he went immediately to do as she said, but Mimie called him back.

"No no," she said, "I'm drunk so muckle tea I'm fit to burst."

"Well sit down a while anyway," Clemmie offered, but Mimie would not be persuaded.

"Na, lass," she said, "I'll just go home. I have to get used to him no being dere."

And despite Clemmie's concern, she went next door to the old croft house of Wurlie, where the Raeburn was out and the rooms cold and she was alone.

"Well," said Albert, "what did the doctors have to say?"

Clemmie saw the whisky bottle on the sideboard and crossed the room to the half-finished flask which she silently replaced in its cupboard. She shut the sideboard doors, and stood with her back up against them, as if trying to prevent Albert from drinking any more.

"He's fractured twa vertebrae in his back."

"Christ!"

"And his skull. That's besides the concussion and the fact he's no youth anymore," she explained.

"Christ!" he said again.

Clemmie sat down in the seat next the fire. She held her hands out to the peat embers smouldering in the hearth.

"Poor Mimie," she sighed.

Albert stood staring blankly into space for a moment, then unconsciously crossed to the sideboard and poured himself another whisky.

Clemmie watched disapprovingly, but said nothing.

Albert sipped the glass of golden liquor thoughtfully.

After a time, Clemmie spoke.

152

"Did da bairns go off to bed all right?"

"Ja, finally. Dey kept asking where du was."

"And did du tell dem?"

"I said du was in Lerwick wi Mimie."

"About Lowrie, I mean?"

"No," Albert mouthed, "I thought we'd leave it till we kent how he was."

She snapped angrily at him. "I wish du'd take some responsibility Albert. Dey're dy bairns too."

Albert's face fired red. "What have I done wrong now?" he boomed.

"Du just doesna want to do anything hard, does du? 'Leave it to Clemmie', dat's dy way, isn't it?"

"Damn it Clemmie, du's wrong!" he roared, jumping forward from the sideboard, and as he did, so he spilled some of the whisky over the leg of his trousers.

"Ach!" he shouted, out of frustration, and stomped out of the room.

They went to bed in silence. When Albert's rough hand touched her shoulder, she groaned, pretending to be asleep.

•••

The next few weeks were tense ones at Glimmerwick. Mimie could hardly believe how lonely she was without him, and for a fortnight she moped about the house, unable to do anything. She took every opportunity to go to Lerwick, as much to escape the house as to check on Lowrie's progress.

Albert grudgingly went about the crofting jobs, quiet and sullen, with a bottle never far from his hand. He avoided the subject of who would run the crofts in the future, trying desperately to ignore the facts of the matter, that the responsibility landed squarely at his door.

Clemmie responded to being needed. She almost seemed to enjoy this chance to be of service to her neighbour, and kept a close watch on Mimie.

The bairns sensed what was afoot, although they were not

informed of the details. Isaac helped his father around the croft without being asked, but Ellen was not used to being out of the spotlight and did her best to be a burden. The atmosphere was decidedly strained, not assisted by the weather which was consistently wet and windy.

The Butlers too were in a state of flux, Oliver having had an interview for a new post in London and now impatiently waiting on news of his application.

Perhaps Lowrie was least affected by all the changes taking place. Once the concussion passed, he soon came to terms with his injuries and was the darling of the nurses with his kindly manner and droll humour. Only the crippling boredom really hurt him, that and the fact that he would miss the lambing for the first time in almost thirty years.

•••

He placed the round wooden draught on the cardboard check with a click and lifted three of his opponent's pieces he had captured. One single white draught remained, surrounded by the force of Lowrie's crooners. His opponent, the thin man who occupied the bed next to him on the ward, looked at Lowrie with an admiring smile.

He moved his last remaining piece towards the inevitable capture.

"Another game?" he asked with a lower lip that quivered.

Lowrie gazed for a moment at his thin face and shook his head. They'd played five games of draughts already that morning and Lowrie had won them all without the slightest effort. He yawned and the striped hospital dressing-gown fell loose over his bony shoulders, then began stacking the draughts back into their tattered box. His fellow patient stammered.

"Du's brawly good at draughts, man," he said, repeating the statement he had made after all the previous games.

Lowrie smiled. "We used to play at da whaling, on board ship," he explained. "You get to ken da right moves."

He placed the lid on the box, wheeled his chair over the tiled floor to the cupboard where the games were kept, then returned to his companion. He looked out through the day-room windows to the cliffs of Bressay and Noss. To Lowrie, these represented freedom.

"It's a long day in here," he observed.

"I-I-I'm been here six months. You get used to it," the thin man answered. Lowrie moved in his wheelchair, his body cringing away from the pain that was now a familiar part of his life. He grunted as a stabbing knife twisted in his back.

"Shite!"

But even though the pain was more intense when he was out of his bed, he had spent so long confined to the iron-framed prison that he willingly took the chance to get up and use the wheelchair.

Bert, as his acquaintance was known, was a pensioner from the south end of the islands. He nodded to the other people sitting in the day-room.

"Some o dem are hardly here at all," he said without a stammer.

And he was right. Most of the old folk there had little knowing of their location. They seemed divorced from reality. One old woman, known simply as Bessie, sat wizened in her orthopaedic chair watching them. Her head moved in an ugly twitch.

"Whit's dat? Whit are you saying aboot me?" she cackled.

Her ashen face shrivelled into lines of fear and anger.

"Nothing, Bessie," Lowrie replied, but she eyed him suspiciously before drifting back into her youthful sanctuary. "Is dere any bread in da press?" she would cry out, without any warning, and the nurses would have to assure her that there was plenty of food in her house. At other times she would manoeuvre her arthritic old frame through the corridors, then squat down and urinate on the polished floor.

"Damn it," Lowrie growled, "I'll have to get out of here. I'll go daft afore long."

Bert shook a cigarette from the single pack he made last him a week, and kindly offered one of the precious filters to Lowrie's fingers. Lowrie refused. Bert lit his smoke with a shaky hand. He sucked it deep into his lungs, then broke into a retching cough.

"I'm supposed to give dem up," he spluttered, making it obvious why, "dey say it'll kill me . . ."

Lowrie looked at him.

"But I say what's da point? I've naebody, nae family, nae reason to care."

He drew hard on the cigarette again.

"When I was a boy, du wasna a man if du didna smoke. And now dey tell us d-d-dat it'll kill wis."

Bert shook his head slowly from side to side, smoke issuing from the sides of his quivering mouth.

"D-d-da thing is, dey'll not come right out and ban it. No. D-d-dere's too much money in it for da government."

He wheezed again. Lowrie wasn't listening. He was watching an oil supply boat head out the south mouth of Lerwick, the south mouth which had given its name to the dialect term for an incomer: soothmoother.

"It all changes," Bert went on. "Us auld folk, we can't keep up wi it. We just get left ahint."

Lowrie had had enough of his chatter. He just quietly closed his eyes and shut himself off. Bert hardly seemed to notice. Probably he was used to talking to more senile minds. He carried on his monologue on the changes. He gave his views on oil, incomers, modern music, hairstyles — anything that seemed to him to somehow symbolise the new ways that so confused him.

"Does du have any bairns?" he asked Lowrie finally. Lowrie opened his eyes.

"Yes, but dey're both in Canada. We've been across for a holiday. Dey asked us to stay, but . . . I could never live dere."

Bert was already on to another subject.

"And dis new currency, dat's another thing," he went on, "what was wrong wi da old money I'll never ken. . . ."

•••

Lowrie was sleeping during the visiting hour, this being one of the days when there was no bus from Hillswick. He hadn't expected any visitors. He was surprised, then, to have his gentle sleep broken by the sound of someone calling to him, and to feel fingers shaking at his shoulder. At first he thought it was a nurse.

He opened his eyes, tried to concentrate. There was a girl smiling down at him, with moonish eyes wide open. She was familiar . . .

"Linda!"

He sat up in bed and reached for his spectacles. As he did so, a twinge of pain shot through his body.

"Damn!" he shouted.

Linda's face became concerned.

"Here, let me . . ."

She passed him his spectacles from the bedside table.

"Linda!" he said again. "It's so long since I saw de. Nearly two years."

She blushed.

"I'd have come earlier but . . ."

"Och, dat's all right, du's here now."

Silence. She sat down alongside the bed.

"And how is your back?" she asked at last.

"Och, no too bad. It's slowly improving. I'm still in a wheelchair, though . . ."

He tried to move in his iron bedstead cage, then looked up at her.

"Could du move my pillows a bit?"

"Of course."

She did so, and Lowrie raised himself until he could see her more comfortably.

"So," he said, "what's du been doing since we last saw de in Glimmerwick?"

She shrugged. "Since I got made redundant at da camp, I've been unemployed most of the time. There's not much work . . ."

He nodded.

"And is du happy, lass?" he asked her, quite directly, in a straightforward manner of his that she had all but forgotten. His old grey face became a reminder of all the time that had passed since she was young and used to sit on his knee in the but end at Wurlie. Time which had intervened between that moment and this suddenly slipped away and he looked kindly at her.

"Is du happy?" he had asked, and something in his face forced the truth from her, though normally she would have deflected such a personal question away from her tongue.

"I suppose so," she answered. "It's my life, after all, Lowrie, if I don't like it, how can I like myself?"

He nodded, and seemed impressed by her reasoning.

She surprised herself with her reasoning too, and glanced around her to see if anyone else was listening. Nobody was. She turned again to the old face cushioned by pillows.

"But it's *your* health and happiness I'm concerned with, Lowrie. Is there anything I could get for you? Anything you're needing?"

Lowrie shook his head.

"Thanks, but no." He sighed, tired and needing sleep.

"Mimie brings in everything I need."

Linda was aware then of how old Lowrie had suddenly become. Sympathetically she leaned over to his bed and whispered.

"You look tired. I'll go now. But I'll come again when I can."

He looked up from the pillows and smiled. She would come again! He closed his tired eyes and started to dream about his sheep. Linda stood up and left his bedside. As she went to the entrance to the ward, the thin man in the bed next Lowrie's woke up and stared at her.

•••

"Oh he's making rare progress, far better dan I ever hoped for."

Mimie a'Wurlie felt the mouthpiece of the phone moisten with her own breath.

"But it'll be a long time before he's walking again. Still, it's a mercy he didna hurt himsel more."

All the way from Canada, her son's voice wriggled along the miracles of science, till it reassembled in a human form in her ear.

"Oh I'm glad, Mam. Have they told you when they might let him out?"

"Well, nothing definite. But we're hoping it'll no be too long."

She was keeping her two sons up to date with their father's progress by means of regular phonecalls. They could afford the reversed charges, with their practices doing so well.

She said her goodbyes, promising to call again soon. Outside the sun was shining, throwing beams of sunlight into the but end of Wurlie through the small sash window. She sighed, feeling all alone, and thinking how far away the boys were. Until she actually made the journey to Canada herself, Mimie had never quite understood the vast distance between them. Certainly, she knew well enough from maps of the world how great the distance was, but that was a paper measurement, which gave no indication of a human being's reaction to a journey of that length.

They had their own lives to lead, far away from Glimmerwick. They couldn't be expected to drop everything and fly across the Atlantic just to hold her hand. And anyway, Lowrie was on the mend now. In a very short time, he would be home.

Clemmie entered through the front porch.

"Another lovely day," she greeted Mimie.

"Isn't it? Will du have a cup o tea?"

Clemmie said yes and sat down at the kitchen table. While Mimie made the tea, she recounted all the news she had gleaned from her son. Clemmie listened. Their relationship had changed since Lowrie's fall.

"I was telling Andrew that Lowrie might be home shortly," Mimie beamed, pouring the steaming tea into cups. "It's such an good news, I can hardly believe it mysel."

"Yes, it is," Clemmie replied, yet didn't feel entirely happy about it. It was selfish of her not to, but she had grown used to Mimie being on her own in Wurlie and quite liked the new closeness they had found.

"And du's been so good to me while he's been away, Clemmie, I wish dere was some way I could thank de."

Clemmie smiled weakly. "Dere's no need for thanks, Mimie; du kens dat."

"Yes, but still, if dere was something I could do."

Clemmie smiled again, and sipped her tea. She didn't want pay. All she wanted was for Mimie to remain as close as she had become of late. But deep inside her, where all truths lie, Clemmie knew that everything would change again.

Two weeks later, Lowrie was released from the hospital. His

injuries had healed surprisingly quickly, and he was able to move about a little on a pair of crutches.

Despite warnings to take it easy, the first thing the old crofter did when he arrived home in Glimmerwick was to visit Albert to get the news from the croft first hand. Albert answered all his questions with short blunt phrases, his face heavy and worried. He fetched a bottle of whisky from the lounge, and insisted on Lowrie's having a drink with him to celebrate his return. Albert had been drinking heavily lately, a mouthful here and a mouthful there, as he had since Lowrie's fall.

In a couple of week his leave would be over, and the matter of the future was weighing on his mind. Lowrie raised the subject in his roundabout way.

"I'll be hard pressed to keep da crofts running, now I've dis things to drag about," he said, indicating the crutches.

Albert's retort was sharp.

"I'm not a bloody crofter, Lowrie, I'm a seaman. And a damned good one."

His ruddy red face became redder and he began fiddling with the bottle of perfume which he had brought home for Clemmie. A bottle she had never opened.

"Oriental women dab perfume on dir temples," he said, changing the subject. "Dey believe dat's where da strongest body odours come from."

"Is dat right?" Lowrie queried, politely, but puzzled by the relevance of this remark. He glanced at Clemmie, who blushed. Albert sipped his whisky.

"Have another dram, Lowrie," he said. "Aye, funny ideas some o them have."

Clemmie watched him as he reached out for the bottle.

"Does du think du should, Albert?" she asked him. "Du did promise to take Isaac out in da boat."

Albert threw her a lurching look.

"Ach, keep quiet woman," he said loudly with a touch of humour. "Come on Lowrie, I've another bottle in ben. To celebrate dem slipping de."

He tipped the almost empty bottle towards Lowrie's glass.

Lowrie stuck out his hand and tried to refuse, but the whisky poured out, over his hand now covering the glass, and over the linen tablecloth.

"Now see what's done," Albert roared, still in part humour. "Get a cloth, Clemmie."

She did as he ordered silently, leaving the table with a sullen look. Albert refilled Lowrie's glass, this time without objection.

"I must go after dis one," Lowrie compromised.

"Man, du's getting old, Lowrie. Time was du couldn't get enough o dis stuff."

"Ach dat was a long time ago, Albert. We were all younger dan."

"Du spends too much time wi sheep, Lowrie, and no enough wi folk," Albert observed, then guffawed at this joke of his. Neither Clemmie nor Lowrie joined in. Lowrie's face was growing angry, in a slow way.

Finally, he spoke.

"If I was to spend as much time drinking as de, Albert, I'd be a damned poor crofter," he said quietly.

The sea captain in Albert Henry sensed insubordination. His eyes narrowed and his thick eyebrows lowered. There was a moment of anger brewing, then he kicked back his chair, and marched to the door.

"I'm away to Hillswick to da pub. I might find somebody a bit more civil and sociable dere," he announced, then left the room giving Clemmie no time to comment. The front door thudded behind him, and she heard the car start up and drive away, Albert's anger over-revving the engine.

She tried to smile bravely at Lowrie, who was watching her reaction with some worry on his face. She sat down at the table, and said nothing.

"I shouldna have said anything," Lowrie observed slowly. "I didna realise . . ."

Clemmie shrugged.

"It's true, Lowrie, I should have said it mysel long ago."

"Has he been doing a bit o boozing lately, dan?"

"Ach a bit, Lowrie. Du kens how it is wi him, never happy but when he's in a boat."

"Has he tried da lobster creels at all?"

She sighed. What was the point of this questioning? It wouldn't change anything. She knew that Lowrie liked to think of her as his peerie sister, but there was nothing he could do. It was between the two of them, and had to be sorted out within the space between them. She had made the mistake before of consulting other people and knew how Albert reacted to the thought of outsiders poking in.

"He's spoken about it. But dey're all needing mending, and he can't seem to get around to it."

"He's no taken to crofting, I see?"

"No, Lowrie, hardly."

She picked up her knitting and started clicking the needles nervously. She did this without concentrating, in the manner of so many Shetland women, quite able to devote her mind to other subjects while the pattern grew. At this moment, she wished it was not so. She wanted to close her mind to Lowrie's prying presence, well intentioned or not, to bury herself in Fair Isle.

Or did she? She wanted him to go away, yet at the very same time she wanted to be able to open up to him and rid herself of all her troubles. To play the role of younger sister as he directed.

He didn't leave. He watched her. And as the seconds slipped by, her resistance to his attentions waned. She felt as if he were a hoody crow, circling above her expiring pride, yet a crow which would only pick away those parts of her which were dead and rotting.

Then she would be relieved. The skeleton of her secrets would be pure once more, but incomplete. For in the act of letting loose, she also slipped the reins of secrecy which held the bridle of her marriage. It was her problem, hers and Albert's. Not Lowrie's.

She defended.

"I'm all right, Lowrie. Honestly. I ken du's concerned, but I'm all right."

With these words, she reaffirmed what she already knew in her heart. And as the words left her lips, the lifeline thrown to her, the light that had briefly lit her darkness, faded and she was alone again.

•••

Albert left the car at Hillswick. They had a tip-off that the police were waiting at the end of the road ready to catch any drunken drivers. He went with a fisherman who lived nearby and indulged in an all-night drinking session at his house.

In the morning, he woke up on the couch, hungover. He was the only one awake, and slipped out the front door quietly. He couldn't be bothered going back to Hillswick to collect the car, and instead set out walking over the hill to Glimmerwick. It was a fine morning and the heather was in the early stages of bloom.

Where had he been? she would cry. Why hadn't he come home.

Always in at the errors of his ways, like a sheepdog snarling at a hedgehog, wary of the sharp spikes, but angry. So Albert curled in a defensive ball of silence, showing only the sharpest points of his nature. He worked damned hard at sea. He had a right to relax. If he wanted to spend his leave having the odd drink with an old pal, he could. It was his business, not hers. Didn't he provide her with everything she wanted, automatic washing machine, chest freezer, everything. . . .?

He was steeling himself for the reception he would receive. He was twisting things round in his head until she was the guilty party and not he. He watched the sea below him, as it rolled against the rocks in the distance.

"Come away," whispered the sea winds, and he heard them.

It was almost lunchtime when he finally climbed the gentle slope up to Glimmerwick. His legs were aching, and the numerous swigs he had taken from a half-bottle of whisky during the walk had renewed his drunkenness.

Clemmie was in her garden, tending her roses.

His first impulse was to sneak past her and go straight to bed. Then he remembered all the bitterness he'd been working up as he staggered home and decided to vent it on her.

She saw him coming and stood up. She was wearing gardening gloves and had the sun behind her. Albert couldn't see her expression clearly. For a moment, he stood trying to focus on her face. She knew right away that he was very drunk.

163

"Well?" she said, not angrily, but expectantly, awaiting some kind of explanation.

Albert stepped forward.

"I was visiting," he said quite boldly.

"Wha?"

"Jimmy Coutts."

"Dat boozer! I might have kent."

Albert's anger snapped the short distance to his tongue.

"It's my bloody leave. I'll spend it how I want."

She said nothing.

"Have I no done what I had to on da crofts?"

She didn't take up his invitation to argue.

"Do whatever du wants, Albert."

He leapt forward, into battle.

"Jesus Christ, I just don't understand de. One moment du's begging me to bide home and run da croft, and next . . ."

He ran out of words and stammered furiously for a second.

"Dan du's telling me to do what I want!"

But the words didn't come out as he wanted and frustration welled inside him.

"Albert," she said quietly. "I'm sick of this."

She stooped to snip at one of her roses.

"Sick of drinking, of de, sick of de getting too drunk to do things that du has promised."

She gazed up at him with sadly vexed eyes.

"Did du forget du promised to take Isaac out in da boat dis morning?"

Steaming with a hot boozy rage, he bellowed.

"Where is he? I'll take him out!"

"Keep dy voice down, Albert," she hissed. "Mr Butler's over washing his car. He'll hear . . ."

"I don't care," he replied, still shouting. "I'll take him out in da boat like I promised. Where is he?"

She snorted, mockingly.

"Du'll take him nowhere. Not in a state like yon; du'll drown both o you."

Albert exploded. How dare she belittle his ability to handle a boat, drunk or sober? He with a master's certificate? He leapt forward and gripped her thin wrists in his fleshy hands. In fright, she struggled to free herself, but the harder she struggled the tighter he held her, till her arms hurt.

"Let me go, Albert. Please."

But he just stood there, glaring at her, his red face even redder and his eyes like lights, with a half-crazy smile on his lips.

"Let me go, Albert, I'm warning de!"

And with that, she loosed a sharp kick to his shins, which made him release her left arm. She pulled away from him, and as she did so, the point of the secaturs in her hand cut his wrist. He released entirely and stood staring in horror at the wound.

"Du's cut me, Clemmie," he said in disbelief.

She dropped the cutters, forgetting her passion.

"Albert, I'm sorry, I didna mean to . . ."

"Du's cut me," he said again, suddenly like a little boy.

She led him into the house and bathed then dressed the wound, no more than a scratch, really, but to Albert's mind a symbolic gash of great depth. It seemed to bring him to his senses somehow. She made him black coffee and sat down with him. He had gone a deathly shade of pale and looked ill. He stared at her for a long time, still wearing his boyish look of fright, then with a sigh he lowered his eyes and gave her a weak smile through the bush of his beard, as if realising the truth of their circumstances.

"Clemmie, I just . . ." he began, "I mean I want to do what du wants, but it's hard for me. I ken du wants me to stay at home and run the croft and work at Sullom Voe and all, but I just don't ken if I can. I'm a man that likes a routine. I'm used to sailing . . ."

She shrugged.

"Du doesn't have to stay at home for me, Albert. I'm just beginning to realise myself that maybe I've been looking for something in de dat isna part of de."

He shook his head.

"No . . ." he began again, but she interrupted him.

"Go back to da sailing, Albert, I'll be all right."

He shook his head again.

"I just don't understand de, Clemmie. I swear I never will."

"Dere's nothing complicated about me, Albert. Du seems to think I'm some kind o puzzle. But I'm no really . . ."

"No?" he said seriously.

"No, really. I'm just a person, flesh and blood. Du seems to think I'm like a piece of machinery, like a . . . a clock or something, du can take it apart and see what makes it tick, dan put me back together again. But I'm no clock, I'm more like a . . . well I'm just a woman, Albert, a person, same as de."

He said nothing, simply stared at her with his dark eyes, hidden under furled brows. She went on, trying to explain herself better.

"I'm a living thing, like a rose. Du can't take a flower apart, petal by petal, and see why it's bonny. All du would be left with is a bare stalk. And dat's me, Albert. Du can't take me apart and still be left wi Clemmie. All du'll have is a thin stem, and no bloom. Just take me as I am, don't try to understand me. God kens I have to do it wi de."

Albert tried to comprehend the truth in her words. He tried to curl his rational mind around her imagery. After sitting for a time stone-faced, staring at his coffee cup, as he held it between finger and thumb, as if aware of the minute size of the grain in her truth, she could almost hear the motions of his mind.

Suddenly he leapt from his chair.

"Poor bloody martyr! Poor bloody martyred Clemmie!" he bellowed. "Just listen to Clemmie wi her hard, hard life . . ."

Then he leaned close, bending forward till his big face blotted out the light.

"Does du think it's one long foy being married to de?"

With that, he stormed out of the bungalow, slamming the door behind him. Clemmie sat motionless, angry with herself. She had come so close to penetrating the gulf that separated them. But the words had failed her. She began to cry, slow sad sloth-like tears that were shaped like dewdrops. He had pulled the bloom from her. Now only the bare stalk remained.

•••

Albert walked angrily away from the house. He stopped in the middle of the tarmac turning place. He could see right out to the Atlantic from there, to the solitary reef of Muckle Ossa lying off the coast. The boozy fire raged hot in him. Why did she have to belittle him all the time? At every turn, she had to make some remark about her life with him and how terrible it was. Did he not provide a decent modern dwelling, and money for all she needed? Surely he wasn't the person she made him out to be, always selfish and ogreish, forcing her to bow and bend to him?

Oliver Butler was waxing his car. He saw the bearded figure standing only a few yards away and with the noonday sun in his eyes, it seemed as if Albert Henry was making some kind of motion towards conversation.

"Morning," said Oliver Butler, in a friendly cheery voice. He had received news that morning of the job in London he was after, and his temper was as good as the news.

Albert grunted in surprise. He didn't like the Butlers, and what they stood for, the affluence of oil, and their status. In the past he had kept his distance from them.

"Another nice day," Oliver continued. "This weather is a pleasant surprise." He applied a little more wax to the wing of his Ford Granada. "On days like this, I almost regret that we're leaving."

Albert grunted again, in some surprise.

"Going?"

"Yes, I just found out this morning."

"Found out what?"

"About my new post — in London."

"London?"

"Promotion — to the head office," Oliver Butler disclosed, with a smile of self-satisfaction. In his present mood he was feeling quite expansive — he liked to talk about his career, especially now that it had taken a new turn upwards.

Albert walked over to the red Ford, forgetting Clemmie for a moment, but not his annoyance.

"Weel," he said slowly, with a look of mischief on his face, "you were only here for da money after all. We all kent you'd go when da money stopped. It's not as if you loved da *place*, like a Shetlander . . ."

Oliver was a little surprised by this tone. He raised his eyebrows.

"Well, no, but you're not being quite fair, I mean . . ."

Albert interrupted.

"Fair?" he said. "Nothing is ever fair, Mr Butler."

He took the half-bottle from his hip pocket and unscrewed the top. He offered it to Oliver Butler. The bottle contained only an inch of golden liquor. Oliver politely refused this fumbled gesture of friendship.

Albert turned to the impressive structure of the Haa House, once the home of the laird and ruler, now a status symbol for these wealthy strangers.

"No doubt you'll be making a fat profit on da hoose," he said.

Oliver raised his eyebrows again.

"Actually, I haven't found a buyer yet. But it hasn't been on the market long."

He looked hard into the bloodshot eyes of Albert Henry and saw the anger still burning in them from his earlier battle.

Oliver cleared his throat.

"Don't suppose you'd be interested yourself?" he asked, half in jest, trying to lighten the tone of things.

"No. Definitely not." Albert's face lit again with that look of mischief. "I mean, it's no a house for a common seaman, captain or no. It's a gentleman's house, isn' it?"

Again he offered the whisky bottle. Again his gesture was refused.

"Gin and tonic man, I suppose," Albert leered. "All G&Ts, is it? G&Ts and *Horse and Hounds* and *Country Life*. See, I do ken something about your kind."

Oliver was sharp to the game now.

"Having a little dig are we?" he said, standing up.

"Dig? What would du ken about digging? Du wouldna ken one end o a spade from da other!" he snorted scornfully, and slugged from the half-bottle. Then he turned to his neighbour with a sly grin.

"Ken what I reckon? I reckon Shetland was better off without you and your damned oil before you came, and it'll be a better place when you've gone . . ."

Oliver started to reply then hesitated. He thought for a moment how he should handle the situation.

"Possibly that's true," he said slowly, "but there have been benefits, even you must admit."

"Benefits! Benefits? You come swaggering in here, destroying what's been a unique way o life for decades and you tell me there's been benefits? You've spread your damn money about, taken folk away from da traditional industries, upset everything that made Shetland what it was, and you say there's been benefits?"

Oliver said nothing. He met Albert Henry's glare with a look of measured resistance.

"You really are spoiling for a fight, aren't you?" he said quietly. "Do I detect a little chip on your shoulder, perhaps?" he questioned with a humourless smile on his round face.

Albert stood with his mouth open a fraction, his head tilted slightly back, an aggressive focus in his eyes. Then he laughed, but it was a laugh which concealed a great deal.

"No, not me, Mr Butler. You see, I've nothing to envy you for. I'm all right. But you're right in saying that there's a lot of folk in Shetland that do have a chip on der shoulder. And quite rightly too. You see, Shetland was ignored by you and your kind for decades. For decades, the only way for a young man to make anything o himsel was to go to sea or to emigrate. Now why was that? I'll tell you. Because until they discovered oil in the North Sea, not one o you bastards down in the south of England gave a damn about Shetland. Most o you didn't even ken where it was! You were quite happy to take whatever we produced for a mere pittance, be it knitwear, fish, wool, whatever, even just plain human talent — for there was many a Shetlander left the islands who went on and did well for himself in other places. The world is full o them. But few o them came back. Because there was nothing here for them. For years the best brains and the folk wi real drive have been forced to move away to get on, because your glorious government didn't have the slightest interest in investing any money up here to provide a few real jobs. All we've ever had is bureaucracy. No commerce."

Albert stopped. He was surprising both himself and Oliver Butler with his eloquence. He took a sip from the whisky, then drained the bottle and threw it from him.

"But," he went on, "as soon as dere was something in it for them, like now, wi the oil, there's no thought for man nor beast as might happen to live here, it's get the money fast as they can and go . . ."

Oliver Butler applauded ironically.

"Bravo," he said. "A fine speech. I'm converted to your cause, where do I sign?"

Again Albert's beard shook with contempt.

"My cause would never take your kind . . ." he whispered in a bitter breath.

Oliver reached breaking point. He had taken as much as he could. He threw down his wax-covered rag.

"Now look here. You keep referring to 'my kind' as if I'm part of some class of untouchables. I've lived here for two and a half years, and before that in Voe, and I haven't had the slightest trouble with anyone. I haven't usurped anyone. I'm just doing my job, living my life. And I don't owe you any explanations. . . ."

The balance of power had shifted. It was the oil man's turn.

"That is, until you come wandering over here, shouting. Whatever happened in Shetland in the past has nothing to do with me. Maybe you have had a raw deal. I don't know. But in the past few years, oil has brought a great deal of money to Shetland. We employ young Shetlanders at the terminal, you know, we give them a chance to stay in the islands.

"And come to think of it, it's just as likely to my mind that it's your 'kind' that are to blame for the fact that so many people have left Shetland in the past, driven away by your petty-minded boorishness!"

Albert was speechless. He had already said everything he could.

"So if you don't mind, I'd like to finish polishing my car and enjoy the rest of what was a very pleasant day till you arrived. All right?"

A soprano handclap broke out behind them. They turned to see Joan Butler standing in the doorway of the Haa House with a smile of admiration on her.

"Well spoken, Ollie," she squeaked in a high-pitched voice. "I'd never have believed you had it in you." She walked forward till she stood by her husband's shoulder.

"And as for you," she said to Albert, "I can only say you may have saved a middle-aged marriage from foundering on the rocks of indifference."

She took her husband by the arm.

"Come along Ollie," she said, beaming.

Albert was left staring at the two of them as they walked towards the open door of the Haa House.

Oliver stopped and glanced back at the bearded seaman as he entered the house.

"If I were you, I would drink less," he said in an even tone.

Under his breath, as the door closed, Albert breathed heavily.

"You'll see. We'll no take your shite forever . . ." he said, then turned and left the Ford Granada still half-waxed in the turning place before the old laird's home.

•••

Clemmie was preparing the lunch, crying as she did so. She started slicing onions to disguise her tears from the children. A feeling that it was all too late had taken hold of her. She was lost in her own kitchen.

Ellen, her daughter, entered the room.

"Onions," sniffed Clemmie, "always make me greet."

Ellen said nothing. She sat in her father's chair, looking huffy. After a time Clemmie asked her what the matter was.

"It's daddy," the girl said, annoyed. "He won't take me out in the boat."

"Daddy's not going out in the boat, darling," her mother replied.

Ellen insisted. "He is. He's gone and taken Isaac wi him."

Clemmie almost fainted. Her head pounded with a pulse of dread.

"When did they go?" she asked in a breath of whispered fear.

"Ten minutes ago or so. I was down at the boat wi them, but Daddy wouldna take me. I hate him sometimes . . ."

Clemmie had no thought for teaching her daughter respect. Her mind fell into a wild panic and she dashed from the room, dropping a half-peeled onion and her knife on the lino floor. Ellen went after her, calling out.

"Mammy, Mammy, what's wrong?"

Clemmie couldn't reply; in her mind's panic she saw the rowing boat out in the middle of Glimmerwick, with Albert drunk and angry and her small son so afraid and calling out for his mother. Albert had no closeness with the children. He was little more than a bringer of gifts to them. If Isaac grew scared, Albert wouldn't know how to handle the situation, and in his drunkenness God only knows what might happen.

All these thoughts sped through her mind as she ran from the bungalow followed by her daughter shouting 'What is it?' at the disappearing heels of her mother.

Clemmie crossed the turning place till she could see the bay below. She put her hands to her face to shield her eyes from the bright sun, and scanned the water slowly, biting her lip as she did so.

"What is it, Mammy?" Ellen cried again as she caught up with Clemmie.

Her mother sighed.

"Daddy's drunk . . ." she answered, tired of hiding the truth.

"He's always drunk," came the tiny voice, but Clemmie didn't hear. She methodically searched the sheltered water of Glimmerwick and saw no sign of the boat.

"God save us, he's no taken him out bye, has he?" she whispered and turned her eyes towards the narrow neck of the voe where the force of the ocean crashed and rolled and chewed. Beyond the bay of Glimmerwick there was no shelter from the Atlantic. It was impossible for Clemmie to be sure. Her eyesight was not as sharp as it once had been. She felt a heavy lump swelling in her throat. Her mind formed the picture of the overturned rowing boat and its helpless occupants now clinging on for dear life to an oar or a wooden fishbox while the waves kept thumping down on them, each crashing blow loosening their grip further until . . .

She couldn't be sure. It was too far away. She turned and ran to the nearest house, Wurlie, and burst through the door just as Lowrie and Mimie were sitting down to eat their lunch of salted piltock and potato.

"Lowrie, Lowrie, gie me dy glesses," she cried out.

Lowrie looked at her for a moment in surprise, then seeing the seriousness of Clemmie's mood, he rose from the table and moved quickly across the room to where he kept his binoculars.

"Lass, what's wrong?" asked Mimie.

"Albert! Albert's wrong. He's drunk and he's gone out in da boat wi Isaac and I can't see dem anywhere. I think he's gone out bye . . ."

She took the binoculars and dashed outside again. Lowrie and Mimie followed. Clemmie scanned the distant water.

"Can du see dem?"

"No . . . no, wait, here's something . . ."

"What is it?"

"It's a boat. I'm no sure if it's them. Now . . . no, it's not a boat. Damn . . ."

She scanned the coastline carefully, the lump in throat growing larger and larger the longer went by. Finally, she gave up and handed the glasses to Lowrie.

"Du look," she said, "I canna bear it . . ."

She turned away as Lowrie calmly took the glasses and moved slowly from left to right of the watery vista, searching for the small boat.

"Damn it, damn him . . ." Clemmie whispered. "I told him no to."

Lowrie handed the glasses to Mimie and shook his head from Clemmie's distress. Mimie began looking. Lowrie put his arm around his neighbour and tried to comfort her.

"Albert'll be all right, Clemmie. He kens what he's doing in a boat. Ever since he was a boy coming here for holidays, he's been . . ."

"He's drunk," Clemmie cried out, "drunk!"

Lowrie sighed.

"Please, Lowrie, believe me, phone da coastguard."

"And what'll I tell him, dat dere's a man wi a master's ticket out in a rowing boat?"

"Lowrie!" Mimie warned, "she's right. Phone."

"Please," begged Clemmie.

Lowrie gave a solid grimace, and waited.

"Please," she said again.

He sighed and turned towards the house. He was about to agree when a car suddenly appeared over the brow of the hill of Glimmerwick. Everybody turned to look. It was Albert and there was Isaac waving out the passenger door window. Clemmie turned to her daughter.

"Ellen! Du said he'd gone out in da boat."

"He did!" She pointed to the small noost below. "See, da boat's no dere."

The car stopped and Isaac jumped out. He ran across to his mother, calling out to her happily . . .

"Daddy didna forget! He did take me out in da boat!"

Clemmie's head was still spinning but now it was with relief.

Albert got out of the car, still looking red-eyed and drunk. He grinned a little sheepishly through his thick beard.

"We just rowed across da voe, dan I got Jimmy Coutts to give me a lift to Hillswick to get da car."

For a minute everybody was silent. Then Lowrie smiled and his smile turned into a laugh. The little boy looked up at the old crofter and started to laugh too, though he did not know why. Then Ellen laughed too, and Mimie, then Albert, and finally Clemmie herself.

"I'll go and phone da coastguard dan," Lowrie said through his humour, and the laughter increased to a fever of nervous relief.

Albert put his arm around his wife. As Lowrie and Mimie went back to the house of Wurlie to eat their now cold lunch, he whispered in Clemmie's ear. He spoke only two more words but they were musical and magical to her mind . . .

"I'm sorry . . ." he said.

•••

At the annual regatta that year, Albert Henry and his crew won almost every cup on offer. It was a feat unequalled in the regatta's history and became the talking point of the district.

At the dance which followed, when the trophies were presented, Clemmie held her head high. She had never really liked this sort of social gathering in the past — often because Albert was away at sea and she had no partner. This year, with him triumphant on the water and sober too, she enjoyed herself.

She wore a silk dress which her husband had brought home from the sailing for her — or rather, a silk dress which she had made from the material he had given her. But it looked as if it had been bought from an expensive shop, and Clemmie never gave her secret away.

Halfway through the night, the club president's wife came across and sat down beside her. She complimented Albert on his winning ways, then spoke quietly to Clemmie.

"What a lovely dress!" she remarked, and her spindly fingers took hold of the material on its sleeve.

"But so thin!" she went on.

Clemmie looked at her with an air of self-assurance she hadn't often used before.

"It's the last silk dress I'll ever have, less he buys them in Lerwick," Clemmie said, more to Albert than the woman. "He's got a job as a pilot at Sullom Voe."

Albert nodded. He looked happier and healthier than at any time in the previous ten years and was sober too despite the drinking going on about him.

"Aye," he said, "it's a wrench. But I realise how much da bairns need me home, you see. And Clemmie too, for dat matter."

The president's wife nodded in return. She was surprised to say the least. Who'd ever have thought that Albert Henry would give up the sailing?

Not one person in Northmavine that knew him.

•••

The Butlers left Glimmerwick in September of 1983. They left

175

behind the Haa house still unsold, its luxurious interior now carefully dismantled, packed away and shipped by ferry to the mainland. Oliver's business nose had let him down. There were no buyers for his country house. Throughout the islands, the property market once (so recently) alive and booming was sliding backwards into a state of recession.

Those who had bought and sold at the right times had made small fortunes during the decade of oil. Those who had not were left, like the Butlers, with something of a ghostly white elephant growing damp and dreary while its market value dropped.

The new laird had gone like the old. The symbols of his affluence he took with him. Except one. The house remained.

Lowrie heaved a long heavy breath of relief. At last it was all over. A new pattern was emerging, a peaceful one. Ten years before, the old crofter had asked a question of himself. He had known the answer all along: "Nothing is ever the same". Yet somehow it was the same. The changes had been harsh and uncompromising, had never halted for ten long weary years. But that same rapidity also meant that everything was quickly forgotten.

Lowrie was an old man now. Even he admitted it. His back gave him constant pain and he stooped still lower trying to compensate. But with grim-faced will to carry on, he went about his routine as he had always done. His trips to Lerwick once a month, his daily chores around Glimmerwick — the burden of which was somewhat lightened by the fact that Albert Henry was at home more; he forced himself to walk these structured paths as he always had, determined to walk them till he died. Indeed, to die walking them.

This land was his.

Lowrie a'Wurlie became, for the last years of his life, the real laird of Glimmerwick. What lay ahead for his estate he could never imagine, for the knowledge that he was a caretaker, a regent, waiting for the time when his faceless successor would come of age was always with him.

What caused him sadness was the fact that he would never pass control to one of his own children. The soil he had given his life to would never know another Manson. He repeated many times the same sad soliloquy.

"Lowrie man, wha tinks du will ever do whit du does? Dis gjiurm in da eart, eekin oot a livin? Dere'll be nane when du's gone. Dis kind o wark will never please da young folk. Da land will grow nothing but tatties and girss. Da hedder will cover it aa. Da corn will never grow in Glimmerwick again."

But even as the old crofter surmised the end of it all, Barbara Glossop and her husband were planning how to use their new croft to its maximum potential, not a million miles away from the township of Glimmerwick. Her methods might not be Lowrie's, but Barbara had the same love of the land. Nothing is ever the same, but something remains. Ideas and emotions.

Talks are about to begin . . . over a lease for the Sullom Voe Terminal. The Shetlanders are fighting for a £10 million deal, but . . . they will find the oil company much more reluctant to shell out than in the past.

With the roads and schools needed by the oil companies, but built by the Shetland Islands Council, now completed and with construction work at the terminal itself now at an end, the council's negotiating position has largely evaporated. And it is facing an oil industry that is reacting to weak oil prices and rocketing exploration costs by seeking any opportunity to cut a few pounds from budgets.

GORDON BREWER, in *The Scotsman,*
15th August 1984.

CLINGING ON

In the spring of 1983, Linda did nothing. She was in no rush to go back to work, and simply enjoyed having time to do things — anything, it didn't matter what. She didn't have any ambitions as such. She spent a great deal of her time quietly reflecting on everything that had happened to her since she left school.

In some ways she was still clinging on to her immediate past, and to the boom itself. So many of the folk she had grown familiar with had left the islands once the money ceased flowing.

Her life took on a new beat, a new rhythm.

She gave up the caravan in Nesting which had been her home since Haggerty left and moved to Lerwick, where she found a small room to rent. It wasn't a home, but then she didn't want one. She wanted a space which was bare and empty so that she could begin to piece a future together. She thought sometimes about reapplying to art school. She still kept the original portfolio she had compiled while at school in the town, and sometimes she would open it and look through the drawings, marvelling at how youthful they seemed to her now. But she knew inside herself that time was against her. She had had her opportunity and had wasted it.

That one road out of Shetland towards academia had evaporated out of sight.

She spent time wandering around Lerwick in the mornings. She didn't like the town in the afternoon, or in the evening, but in the morning there was a certain purpose in people's movements that warmed her. She would walk past the bakery and smell the bread and drift back into her early memories before the death of her father. She would wander down to Victoria Pier where she and Haggerty had spent so much time that first summer when they were working at the fish factory.

Sometimes when she walked about the town, she felt guilty at her own idleness. At others, she laughed and was glad to think that she had no need of work.

Then, by accident, she met Elsie, her old schoolfriend, in a Commercial Street café. Elsie had left Shetland and had now finished her studies at Glasgow School of Art.

She was back in Shetland for a while, she didn't know how long, or really why, except that she felt the pull very strongly. She had a job in a tiny boutinque, also on Commercial Street.

They began to meet regularly for lunch, in the same café. Linda sensed how much they had both changed, yet it seemed that they had taken different routes to the same place. Elsie, by going to the city, and Linda by remaining in her native islands while the city came to her, in the form of Sullom Voe.

Elsie introduced her to a whole new group of friends, young professional people, many of them now returned to Shetland after studies on the mainland. They were very different from the cast of characters which Haggerty had assembled round himself a couple of years ago; the dope-smoking, hard-toking 'mystics' she knew then.

Linda felt more at home among the new group. They were an even mix of Shetlanders and incomers, more or less, and here it seemed to her the two cultures clashing in the oil boom had blended — amongst these educated young, who seemed to her to have escaped adolescence with remarkably few scars despite their apparent desire to snub convention.

At first she was a little reluctant to speak out when in their company. Not that they were in any way clannish. On the contrary she found them very welcoming. They had fun together, something she had had very little of in recent years, despite her youth. There was a lot of drinking done, hectic conversation and dramatic outbursts. Serious topics were under discussion. The politics of the islands, their future. Shetland's potential as a home for their children. And wider matters too, with importance to the country as a whole. And always at the heart of it was culture, art and craft.

She observed them for some time before she began to speak. She understood that here was a very real potential. For the first time, because of the oil, quite a high percentage of the best minds within a generation were allowed the chance to come home to Shetland.

Sullom Voe had bought them a future, and the handling of the boom by the local council had won them capital to invest.

When Linda began to open up and say her piece within the loose forum, she found they listened. She didn't know why they should. They had studied for years to gain their education — she was a product of a very different schooling, one which had never given her much opportunity for serious thought.

She realised then that she had been thinking all the time she was at Sullom Voe. All those silent days cleaning and polishing, all those thoughts that had passed through her head in the previous six years were not worthless, but were in fact quite vital to her present progressive state of mind. Linda's education had followed a very different path from that of her friends, but she *had* learned.

At the heart of her new group of friends was Elsie's boyfriend, Michael. He was an odd character, very tall and thin, with a youthful face and a receding hairline of curly blond thatch. He wore round gold-rimmed NHS spectacles and consequently bore a studious look. He had recently returned to Shetland like Elsie, after gaining his degree on the mainland. She wasn't exactly sure what he'd studied there.

When he was among them, his presence seemed to change the others. He wasn't fun loving, but instead of his adapting to fit in with them, he seemed to demand that they change in order to become more like him. And it happened too. He gently prodded topics towards them, ever guiding the discussion to the conclusions he wanted them to reach.

Linda listened a lot, but didn't join in so much. Often she would grow tired of their words and would switch off, would watch their strangely ape-like mouths moving up and down and would know what they were trying to say. She felt sometimes that she could put into a couple of sentences what they would draw out into hour-long arguments.

She watched as Elsie and the others fell deeper and deeper under Michael's influence, as he drew them into a kind of servitude, until they looked up to him as their leader. Linda was suspicious of him. She suspected him of a secret arrogance which she felt made the foundations of his promises to them weak.

In some ways he reminded her of Haggerty, though they were opposites in terms of appearance. But at times she saw the same dreamy impracticality in his face as Haggerty had worn when he spoke of his croft and his dream of self-sufficiency.

But Michael's plans were very much more worldly.

When he and Elsie parted, seemingly amicably, he did not drift out of the group. Instead he became an ever more regular patron of the café where they used to meet. Sometimes Linda would see him through the window, sitting on his own, surrounded by papers and books, smoking, and she would turn on her heel and walk away. It was not a dislike of him which made her avoid meeting him head on, more an animal notion. He more than any other made her feel odd among them. She found it hard to believe that he was a Shetlander. His mannerisms and speech were strangely alien.

He had a plan. A mission to bring about what he termed 'a mini cultural revolution' in Shetland. He had selected the old steamer store on Victoria Pier as his site. Together they would turn it into an arts centre, catering for all branches, and this place would showcase all the budding talents in the islands.

"Art," he would say, "works in tandem with action for the advancement of society. Art produces the ideas to stimulate the economy. Then these are taken up and put into practice, during which time a new crop of seeds are sown and grow, so that when society has utilised the last crop, another batch is ready. Shetland is ready for its future. We can bring it about. . . ."

It all sounded so good. Everyone nodded and agreed. They could do it, working as a team.

Linda listened, wary of the power he held. She didn't trust him. He was making promises which would not be fulfilled by enthusiasm alone, and she sensed that the others would be hurt if anything went wrong. They were placing too much trust in Michael.

•••

Linda's savings were diminishing. No matter how hard she tried to get used to living off her dole money, she couldn't. £10 here, £20 there — it was easy to spend, far easier than it had been to make. She was growing tired of Lerwick again. And tired too of her new friends — they seemed to talk in circles all the time.

Her visits to their café became fewer. She sold her Mini. The summer was passing quickly and she knew that come the winter she would be in a very tight position if she didn't do something soon. She was fed up drifting. She wanted an aim, a direction, not some dream spoon-fed by Michael or anyone else.

One day it would all change. Again.

And it did. She couldn't remain silent forever. It was the day when Michael produced his carefully drawn plans for the re-furbishment of the steamer store. He had done the work himself, had measured the building and designed a completely new facade made of glass which could be built onto the existing shell. Inside, he had utilised the limited space to create a small theatre and art gallery. It all looked fine on paper. The others grew excited.

Linda said nothing till she was asked. Even when Michael did ask, she declined to comment at first. But he pressed her, and so she told him.

"You're wasting your time."

Everyone looked at her in horror. She blushed a little. Michael asked her once more what she meant.

"It's silly. You're being stupid and impractical. The building's not even yours and you're making all these plans. You'll just be disappointed. You're all just dreaming — you'll be let down."

This talk was sacrilegious to the rest of the crowd. They began to make sounds of protest. Linda glanced nervously at Elsie but she too was frowning.

Michael stared at her with a strange smile on his mouth which was like a dog baring its teeth. She felt them closing in on her, her guise stripped, her mask of union with them torn from her face.

"It's just that . . ." she went on, "nobody listens to you, because nobody could ever ken what you're trying to say. You just go round and round in circles, so busy in what you're doing that you never notice you're going no place."

Their anger grew louder.

"Art!" she said. "Nobody in Shetland cares about art. You'll need money for this, and where'll you get it? You're just wasting your time," she blurted out, but no one was listening, they were all too angry at her. She rose up and grabbed her coat, on the point of tears, and went out into the street where faces stared at her blankly, without malevolence.

She walked aimlessly down Commercial Street for a while, internally crying at herself, while gazing into shop windows without seeing. Why had she spoken like that to her friends?

Then she heard the sound of someone calling her name and the step of feet running behind her. She tried to hide in a shop doorway but she was too late.

Michael came running towards her. He stopped at her side panting.

"Linda," he said, "we're sorry. Come on back."

She shook her head.

"You're sorry? No, Michael, it's me that's wrong. You do whatever you want."

"No, but you were right to speak. If that's what you felt."

She hesitated.

"It is . . .."

She turned away from him and continued walking down the winding main street. He stood and watched her go, then walked slowly back to the café and his friends.

Linda went home to her one-roomed sanctuary. She sat down on the bed and stared for a time out the small window. Over the tops of the houses she could see the harbour and Bressay in the distance. The *St. Clair* steamer was in town, berthed at the terminal in Holmsgarth. Its blue and white hull illuminated an otherwise grey day, and her eye was drawn to it. There *was* an escape route. The steamer could take her away. In the morning she would wake up in Aberdeen and Shetland would be behind her.

But it wasn't as simple as that. She was connected to her home by a kind of cord which couldn't be seen, an invisible umbilical which had not yet been cut, despite all the changes, despite her new-found self-confidence.

She knew life in Shetland inside out. But she didn't know the place itself. At school, her history lessons had been confined to Scottish kings and queens and the goings-on at court and in battle. She knew more about England and the continent than she did of Shetland's past.

Over the next few weeks Linda put time and energy into her quest for Shetland's history. She went to the local library and museum, to the archives, in search of something she wasn't quite sure of. Somewhere the answer lay waiting, the definitive statement of her belonging, the key to her reason for being. It was something she shared with all Shetlanders, she knew, but also something personal to each and every one. Even Michael and his band of dreaming friends.

The unwritten history of the islands, hinted at in kirk records and in scholarly treatises — the history of how it was to live there, for the common man, not the laird.

Somewhere, the key lay waiting for discovery.

She had found her purpose. She was searching for the heart of ancient Shetland.

•••

Linda stayed away from the café for a few weeks after her falling out. She now knew the kind of Shetland which Michael and his friends were trying to build. And while she understood their motives and appreciated them, she couldn't help feeling that they were blind to certain facts about the boom that were plain to her.

She could remember a time before oil. So faintly that it felt like gossamer, but definitely present, in the ancient rocks and myths. She could hear, as she dipped into the islands' history, the distant skirls of dancers as they whirled in swirling circles to the scraping of the bow upon the fiddle. She could hear the click of heels upon stone floors, the creak of the pump at the well in Glimmerwick where she lived.

But they were threads she could never grasp. And she knew that they would always remain untouchable, except by the gentle fingers of nostalgia. Those childhood days, growing up in the isolated beauty of Glimmerwick, at the end of the road towards the sunset. Next stop Nova Scotia.

What she remembered could have filled a book, a gossamer book connecting those threads of remembered sea and cliffs and beaches, the maas and tirricks. She could recall green summer meadows gripping at the brief summer all-night-daylight with a desperate keenness to live, wild flowers and tiny peaty burns twinkling in the sun.

These she remembered and loved, even though they were untouchable. She knew that they still existed, and to the outsider's eye would appear unspoilt. But in her mind she had ten years of confusion still unsorted in her head, and what lay before seemed very different from what was now there.

Michael and his friends had spent much of the oil era out of Shetland, being educated. They had glimpsed fragments of the time without really seeing. And Linda knew in her heart that all the worthy things they sought to bring to fruition could only materialise when the people of the islands themselves were ready to choose. And before that time would be a time of reflection on the immediate past, a time for sorting out the many changes, for understanding both the wealth and the poverty of the oil decade.

The excesses were over. Money no longer distorted reality. Slowly, Linda and her like were coming to terms with this fact. Once this process was complete then perhaps the new Shetland could be sketched.

But firstly, people would have to admit that the boom was over, would have to cease clinging on to its ghost.

•••

For Linda, that ghost had assumed human form. That of Michael. His exuberant optimism remained in her head long after she stopped attending his informal meetings. It was a stark skeletal contrast to the studies she was now conducting, yet she couldn't seem to shut it out.

As time passed, she began to think that perhaps he had been right. Maybe it was time for the youth of the islands to come out of their closets and contribute fresh ideas — perhaps if they failed to do so now, then things would stagnate and return to the depression of the fifties.

She was well aware of the money that the local council had invested. But money alone could never build the future. Ideas! Enthusiasm! Youth! Slogans for the new prosperity. Progression!

Then, a chance meeting upturned her solitary world of summer 1983.

She had walked up to the Knab, the green headland in the heart of Lerwick which sheltered the harbour from the south. Here old ladies walked their dogs, and children diced with danger on the cliff faces. Here the dead of Lerwick were buried in the cemetery on the clifftop.

She followed the thin tarmac path which skirted the edge of the drop below. She sat on one of the wooden benches there and looked southwards over the water towards Sumburgh Head, where the mainland of Shetland ended in a hump of sudden rock pointing to the outpost of the Fair Isle.

Her mind was far away in the secret Pictish past of her home. She was trying to erase her memory and picture a time before Viking longships brought war to the peace-loving folk who farmed the land and fished in tiny vessels round the coasts.

A voice at her shoulder broke her reverie.

"Linda," it said; the voice of her ghost.

He sat down on the bench beside her. For a while neither of them said anything. Linda had nothing in her mind for him, and wasn't interested in pleasantries or slack talk. The wild treeless land around the small town seemed to open out till it filled a whole universe, a universe in which speech had no place. This ghost sitting next to her was no longer a part of her thought.

Five minutes passed in this vacuum. Then he said . . .

"You were right."

She didn't hear him. She replied in a vacant tone.

"It's all over. There's no point clinging on."

He smiled.

"Sometimes, I waken up in the morning and wonder why on earth I'm back in Shetland after all these years."

187

"So do I," she answered, not to him but to herself. She was thinking of the blue and white ferry which ploughed the waves three times a week.

"When I decided to come back, I thought the young people could start something, something wholesome, solid ideals and enthusiasm. I don't know what led me to thinking that. I just felt it was time to try to do *something*, I suppose."

"So did I," she replied, thinking of her journey without miles at Sullom Voe, and its tiny, highly concentrated city.

"You seemed to sense it. The others, Elsie and all, they took it for granted I knew what I was doing."

"They think you're some kind of saviour," she said, remembering his power over them.

"I never intended for this to happen. I thought it would be different, a shared responsibility. They expect me to lead them to some mystical promised land, like Moses through the desert of culture."

"Can't you do it?" she asked, seriously.

"It's unreal. It's intimidating," was his answer.

She laughed.

"Never trust a ghost. . . ."

•••

She had no control over the weeks that followed. Had she been able to exercise her self-control, she would probably not have seen her ghost again. She was still scared of him, his strange ways, was angered by the way in which he had duped the others into believing in him, and now was running away. But hadn't she known it all along?

Together they travelled all over Shetland. They went to the old ruins at Jarlshof, where centuries of ancient peoples had built settlement upon settlement. They clambered through the tunnels and the roofless stone huts, pretending they were Picts, speaking to each other in a language of grunts, laughing, making love.

They went to the clifftop at Eshaness, near Glimmerwick, dropped stones off the precipitous edge, counted the seconds as they fell. They went camping, had picnics together in heathery suntraps, where colour blazed purple from a million million mauve blooms, and the sweet scent like honey filled their lungs till they almost choked on it. They were young.

It was the most wonderfully foolish time of her life. It made up for every mistake she had ever made. She managed for a few brief weeks to erase all the premature responsibilities she carried forward into her future. But it could not last. It was a dream, a summery illusion, created by their tired minds, which could not by definition survive the autumn.

The end came when he invited her to accompany him on a weekend visit to his parents' home. This came as a surprise to her, as he seemed to have divorced himself from his family entirely.

They were much older than she expected. Real old Shetlanders in the best tradition, like Lowrie and Mimie a'Wurlie. His father had been the local postman before his retirement. He was a kindly man, with a wrinkly face full of laugh lines which seemed to tell many stories he had gleaned in his years of carrying the mail. His mother was a quiet woman, slightly dour, but she too made Linda feel welcome.

She found it hard to believe that these were his real parents. They seemed so different, and looked on him with a benevolent awe which overcame any barriers which might have occurred. They were very proud of his achievements in the academic world. A photograph of him in his mortarboard adorned the mantle.

Yet it was a terribly empty relationship despite all this. And here, in his childhood home, she saw a very different Michael from the one she had first known, and from the other Michael who had come to her secondly, as her lover.

Here he became a dutiful son, polite and respectful. The energetic wildness passed out of him. No longer did he appear alien.

On the Saturday, they walked out over the barren moorland behind the crofthouse, towards the sea and a sandy beach which he knew of. Curlews whooped, lapwings limped away, holding the pretence of a broken wing stiff from them. Michael was strangely subdued. They sat among the heather and ate the tiny bilberries that were ripe and swollen on the feathery green plants which bore them. He poked them into her mouth with a hooked finger, his face full and troubled, about to burst.

"I can't cope with this place, with home," he said, finally, when the silence could not be prolonged any further.

She glanced at him. He was staring out over the moor to the ever present sea.

"Ever since I was a boy, I've had this feeling I was born in the wrong place, at the wrong time," he went on.

Linda lay down in the heather and looked up at the sky. How quickly the clouds appear to move, she thought, how quickly, and how aimlessly.

"We've had a lot of fun, haven't we?" he said in a low voice.

"Yes," she answered, meaning it. Across the moorlands, a few yards away, a hare stopped and pricked its ears up. Michael saw it and clapped his hands. The hare loped slowly off, then stopped again, a little further away. He clapped his hands again, louder, and it hopped off out of sight.

"Why did you do that?" she asked in annoyance. "It was beautiful."

He shrugged. "Why do any of us do anything?"

He rolled over on his back and plucked a thin stem of grass from among the fading heather. He put it in his mouth and started chewing on it.

They lay together, side by side, on the vast moor; together but far apart. His aimlessness could last no longer.

"You're leaving," she said, without sadness.

"Yes," he said; his eyes did not meet hers.

Then she shut him out of her mind. He was only a ghost after all. She listened to the roaring thunder of the distant sea, rushing in and out of her consciousness like a lover, opening up a secret space inside her, with gentle caress.

She thought of all the things she had done, the mistakes she had made, the hours she had lived, and how many of them she had spent inactive. Would she give up all those times she had spent inside that vacant space of hers for some commendation from self-righteousness? Would she ever be able to devote herself to a cause in the way that he seemed to hunger after?

to devote herself to a cause in the way that he seemed to hunger after?

He would do it gladly. And there lay the difference between them. She thought about Michael and his home, about the many changes life had forced him through in the act of educating his alert mind and came to understand the reasons for his strangeness in a clearly defined light. Every step on the road to gaining his degree had stripped a little more of his native identity from him, till there was no way back. He could only then have rejected all that life out of his environment had taught him. Unable to do so, he was now drifting about, at home in no place, not knowing what it was that ailed him, lost in the world which he had so much to offer.

He seemed to sense her thought.

"I can't go back," he said. "I can't cut off my ties with this place, but I can't go back and become the soft-cheeked peerie boy that used to play here. I can't rub out all the places I've seen and the things I've done, anymore than I can my childhood. I'm a mutation. I've got to find something to believe in."

He put his head on his knees, sitting crouched up, as if in mourning. She moved close to him, and kissed his cheek.

"Go," she said, thinking of her mission, of the secret heart of ancient Shetland still undiscovered.

A week later he left.

She walked with him to the ferry terminal, and sensed that this would be the last time she would see him in Shetland. She had contacted one or two of his former followers, to let them know he was leaving, and they had come along to say goodbye. But most of them had gone away as quickly as they came, and only one was walking with them to the dockside.

Michael was wearing a private eye raincoat with the collar turned up and carrying a canvas bag swung across his shoulder. In an effort to cast off the immediate past, he had shaved his head and thrown away the studious spectacles. As they walked, he gradually drew farther and farther ahead, till he was twenty or so yards beyond her. She wanted to run up to him, to kiss him, to tell him he would get there, wherever he was going.

But she knew it was impossible. He was a ghost, bizarre and euphoric, like the decade stretching out behind them.

His one faithful friend said . . .

"Look at him. His journey's started already and we're not with him."

"No," said Linda firmly, "he's a ghost."

GRIND O DA NAVIR

Here, where the great Atlantic
Carves its own poetic statement
In the ancient rocks.
Here, where voices of forgotten memories
Lie concealed in tumbled stones
Once set in worship.
Here, rumours of lost innocence
Riddled with temptation
Tell their tale to the howling gale.

Roofless crofthouses of families scattered,
Their dykes rumbled boundaries
Which no more matter,
Are marks on a map of hidden treasure:
History, unwritten, our secret store
Of priceless measure.

Where is your identity, people of the north?
Where is the definitive statement of your belonging?
Concealed! Concealed, scattered in ruined stone,
A puzzle of spaces in which you have grown.

Here, where the fierce Atlantic
Sculpts the solid wall of cliff.
Here, where the sacred deity of nature
Has its geometric temple.
Here, the rumours of a past innocence
Are buried in a mass of rumbled stone.

The dust was settling, thin on every surface, covering the past like a skin of powdered porcelain.

The oil age highway north from Lerwick to Sullom Voe was no longer busy as a motorway. Many people had left the islands, either willingly with money in their pockets, or sadly, because they had none left. The strain which had threatened to split the seams of the community was gone with them. The slack was being hauled in like sailcloth till the fit was neat again.

"Tinks du will it ever be da same again?"

No, Lowrie a'Wurlie, never the same. But a pale new moon had risen over Glimmerwick, over Shetland, perhaps even the world.

•••

Linda gave her room key to her landlady. They embraced. She was sorry to leave and her face said so. But she had taken all she could out of Lerwick.

The next stage of her journey lay further north, in Glimmerwick. She caught the bus from Lerwick. It was a route she had travelled many times in the past, both as a schoolgirl and as a chambermaid at the workcamp. But now she saw the land with a different eye, closely focused, scrutinising.

She saw in every contour a familiar face which smiled at her. The hills once barren now had personalities as individual as any human, and they happily accommodated any abstract wish she asked of them.

She had studied.

Yet still she knew that she had much more to learn. She knew her purpose now, but it was a crystal orb, swathed in folds of coarse Pictish cloth, and every fold she opened out revealed another. They key to open the door was no modern metal device as it had seemed to be when offered her by the man in the lane.

Glimmerwick greeted her as the prodigal. It welcomed her in, absorbed her. For the first time in her life she lived there in her tiny, isolated, five-house village home, and felt no need of any other place. She was obsessed now with finding out the secret heart. Her purpose.

She lived with Albert and Clemmie and the children for a while. The atmosphere in the house was good. But she made no plans. She could not tell where she might have to travel next. She spent her days walking the land of Eshaness, retracing many of the steps she had taken as a child. It was a wonderful memory, and not only hers. She felt as if she was tapping into some greater memory, shared, a collective unconsciousness which was a valid form of awareness. The ancient feet had left a powerful imprint on this land. She sensed that this place had been revered — the cliffs which edged the Atlantic inspired a form of worship; the sculpture of the coastline leapt out at her from hidden places, calling out 'Here . . . here . . . here . . .'.

"Here we are. Here we are. Look!"

But she could never see them. Somewhere along the line, the link between their time and hers had been misplaced. She knew they were there. She sensed their presence. And she knew that they were angry. Those ancient spirits hiding in the rocks of Eshaness wanted contact, they needed contact, with the living, so that they might be released from their hollow spaces inside the rocks.

The secret heart! If she could only find the secret heart, then she could set them free, and with them all of Shetland too.

How did she know all this? Was she afraid?

No. She was calm. She had killed her own ghosts: the man in the lane, the bizarre spectre of oil. These ghosts would never harm her, they had no need to. They knew that she could help them escape their hollow spaces. They wanted her to. They were waiting, crying out in hollow voices, for her to *see*!

"We are here . . . we are here . . . we are here. . . ."

Voices, like children in the darkness, crying out in fear, begging to be rescued, to be liberated from their darkness, in a warped harmony of unison.

Shetland's past. Lost.

They had no sense of time. They had no idea of how many hundred years they had been locked in their rocks. To them, their fate seemed infinitely void, and they never tired of calling to her. Sometimes at night she would awaken and hear them miles away.

If only she could pinpoint the doorway, then she could unlock them. But how could she do that without the secret heart?

•••

"Linda's been acting funny lately, hasn't she?"

Clemmie looked up at Albert from her chair. He was gazing out the window to the ocean.

"Yes. I noticed. Is she all right, does du think?"

He sighed heavily and stroked his beard.

"I don't ken. I'm worried."

Clemmie was darning a pair of his socks, the seaboot type that he always wore to work — free issue from the company at Sullom Voe.

"I hope she's no on drugs again. I hope no," said Clemmie, shaking her head. "Does du think she is?"

"I don't ken," said Albert. "I don't think so. She seems fine when she's wi da bairns. It's when she goes wandering off on her own, dat's what bothers me."

He was watching the waves breaking on the shore. He had grown used to the new pattern of his life, the shift work at Sullom Voe, and the routine of taking the tankers in and out; but at times the sea winds still called to him.

It could be no other way. But Clemmie was happy and the children too, and that was what mattered. Albert understood now. He understood the particular loneliness of Glimmerwick and the enchantment which accompanied it.

Clemmie knew what was on his mind. She too understood that he would always have times when he felt the pull. But she also knew that he would never go away again. She had won. His other lover, the ocean, had lost him. The light of her youth had been extinguished by time. She was in the middle of a long dark tunnel. But at its end she saw another light, faint, but definitely a light. She didn't know what it was, but she knew one day she would reach it, that it would make her warm and help her see her life for what it really was.

"Ach," said Albert, "I'm no worried about her, no really. I

don't think it's drugs. I think it's just Linda. Just da person she is."

He turned away from the window and sat in his favourite chair: the old resting chair that had been in his family for generations. He tapped and emptied the bowl of his pipe on the arm of the chair, and brushed the charred tobacco into the peat bucket with the back of his hand.

Clemmie watched him with a faint smile on her face, then broke through the thread which she was darning with.

"I suppose so," she agreed.

She wound the remaining yarn into a ball and placed it in a small wicker basket at her side. Albert watched her. She was beginning to put on weight, he thought to himself, but said nothing. He was quite pleased about it really. She had been so very thin for a time. The extra fat seemed to flatter her.

"I was thinking," she said, "how much she's like her mother." Albert nodded.

"Aye, she is." He filled and lit his pipe.

"Du never speaks about her, Clemmie. No since . . ."

He faltered.

"Since what?" she asked, knowing all the time.

"Well, du kens, since she . . .

He hesitated again.

"Since she killed hersel?" his wife said quietly, with no expression on her face.

Albert looked up in surprise.

"Albert, it's no something I want to be reminded o too often. She was my sister. We grew up together. I loved her."

He nodded sympathetically.

"But dat doesna mean I forget. Every day, it's wi me."

He nodded again.

"What about Linda? Maybe she would like to ken."

"She does."

"I mean, more about her. Stories, anything, just anything du can think o."

Clemmie folded up the pair of seaboot socks and placed them on the arm of her chair. She did not look at Albert. She stood up and went to the sink. She stood with her back to him, and began washing her hands. She did this slowly, rubbing soap on them for ages, while the hot tap poured out water which ran away down the drain and into the waste pipes below.

"Sometimes . . ." she began. "Sometimes I think I should tell her, anything, like du says. But other times, well . . ."

She turned the tap off and faced Albert. The hot water dripped from her hands to the floor, making tiny pools on the worn linoleum which had cushioned her feet for years till it was starting to break up and tear off.

Albert waited, anticipating something of great importance. Clemmie looked around at the kitchen as if searching for something. Her eyes were sharp still, but slower moving.

"Does du think we should redecorate in here?" she asked, after a long pause.

He gave a little snort of a laugh through his beard.

"No dis year," he replied, and took a deep draw from his pipe.

•••

Linda spent a lot of time in Wurlie with Lowrie and Mimie, in the evenings after the children had gone to bed. Lowrie would tell her stories from the old days while she listened with wonderment in her eyes. She had overlooked this source of information. He knew far more than she'd ever expected, stories that had been told to him by his father, and probably his father before that. Many of them simply petered out after promising beginnings. Lowrie was apt to wander off onto a different tack altogether if she didn't keep his mind on what he was explaining. But others he related with an element of mystery in his voice which not only kept her interest, but seemed to help him stay on the subject.

He told her about Johnny Notions, as the people called him, who had invented and inoculated the folk around about with his homemade smallpox cure — made on the same principles as modern-day vaccinations were, but years before.

He told her about Magnus Doull of Mirkwick, the man who had been accused of murder and who had been burned in his prison, as everyone thought, before he could come to trial, only to be discovered years later in New Zealand, running a large sheep-farm there, and whose alleged crime was later confessed to by the local factor of the day.

He had hundreds of old stories to tell. She was glad that she had had the chance to hear them now, before they were lost forever, buried along with the old man who was now sadly failing.

It was an important step forward in her quest. Lowrie knew things that were not recorded in any book. So Linda bought a little tape recorder and coaxed him to go deeper and deeper into the past.

Lowrie seemed to relish the opportunity to talk. It was the first time in Wurlie since the coming of the television when conversation took the main role in the evening's entertainment. It reminded him of the old days, of gyaain aboot da night.

Mimie would listen in too, and correct him if he got his facts wrong. She too found his new way of spending the night a welcome change from watching "the box', as she called it.

Although she didn't want to think of it, Mimie knew that Lowrie was ageing fast. It brought tears to her eyes sometimes, to see him struggling to get out of the chair, getting angrier and angrier at his old tired body, still as fiercely independent as he'd ever been, cursing at Nell, his dog, for nothing at all, just to release the tension. Nell too was growing old. She spent most of her time in the house now. At nights, Lowrie let her sleep in the porch, where it was warmer. Her belly hair was grey and she was very overweight with so little work for her to do now that Albert had taken over the day-to-day running of the crofts. He had his own dogs, skittish young things the pair of them, that would snap and snarl at Nell for devilment, because they knew they could get away with it.

Albert had put a lot of money into the crofts. He bought a new machine for turning the hay, another for digging the potatoes, so that no one had to bend their backs. Now the tatties were thrown up onto a conveyor belt contraption attached to the rear of the tractor, and all folk had to do was pick them off that belt, and move them to another at its side. Even Lowrie could help out.

Albert had bought another machine too. For cutting the supply of peats with! This Lowrie could never accept. For him, the tushkar could never be replaced. They had more than a few arguments over it. But Lowrie wasn't fit enough to cut peats anyway. He just stood and watched as Albert drove the tractor up the stony track towards the high ground where the peat banks were, and shook his head.

The peats which the machine produced were more like dog turds. Albert had no understanding of the rituals.

"Dey'll burn just da same in da stove," he would say, and there was no explaining to him the importance of the manner in which the winter's fuel was cut.

Lowrie said no more. The crofts were Albert's now. Lowrie's advice was rarely heeded. Albert had his own notions about managing the land. He was prepared to invest money in order to harvest more. He did not live in harmony with the elements as Lowrie had done. He sought to master them, using technology as his tool.

Lowrie gave a wry smile. Hadn't he been the same with his father years before? And hadn't time reversed his stance? Albert's turn would come, perhaps when Isaac grew to be a man, and Albert's back was bent.

Nothing is ever the same. Change is at the heart of every stalemate. The flames burn out — yet the fire is constant.

•••

Linda was on the verge of understanding. She could sense it. The voices were louder in her mind than ever before, and their calls to her were now more plaintive than at any time.

They seemed to her to emanate from the north-west corner of Eshaness, from the rocky coastline near the Grind o da Navir. This isolated cove had the aura of some form of temple. The rocks there were almost geometric in their patterns, standing straight up in waves of steps, where the folds of geology became vertical. Nature had designed this temple for man to wonder at. It had created an amphitheatre high in the cliff face, which was filled with a pool of stagnant sea water, only refreshed when the fury of the ocean reached a pitch which threw up waves of gigantic proportions. And it had opened up a gate in the cliff face for these waves to enter through, a gate which was bordered on either side by sheer walls of cliff.

The Grind o da Navir.

Linda was drawn to this place by the forces calling her. She would sit in this strange temple, miles from the nearest house, while far below the Atlantic collided with the rock mass. There was great power here. Of all the many wonders of the coastline, this place had been the most revered by the ancients, she felt certain.

She was on the brink of the ocean, and at the same time on the brink of understanding some great secret long forgotten.

Then she had the idea of trying to paint the temple — it seemed to her that she would never understand it simply by being there. As such she was a worshipper, blinded by her faith. Whenever she entered its atmosphere she could no longer rationalise. The sound of their voices became too loud and occupied her mind entirely. But perhaps if she could paint it, then she might be able to use her graphic impressions as a shade to dull its brightness, so that she could see more clearly. Somewhere in the patterns of the Grind o da Navir was the doorway, through which the ancient spirits might be released.

•••

Linda left the bungalow in Glimmerwick with a bag slung over her shoulder. In it she had packed a snack lunch, her box of watercolour paints, paper and brushes. She was ready to begin her preliminary sketches.

She walked down to the shore and along the coastline, humming to herself. It was a strange lament which came from her lips, a melody she had never heard before, but one which seemed in some way to be known to her.

The sun was rising in the summer sky above. Her body trembled slightly in anticipation, not in fear. The ghosts could not harm her. She had prepared herself with great care. She was ready. This would be the day.

The smell of the sea tinged everything — dead tang rotting on the tideline brought the ocean's aroma into the air. It was mixed in with driftwood, plastic flotsam and rusty tins.

Gulls swooped and soared overhead. Arctic terns cried out their high-pitched intentions of war, soprano rattle cries as they prepared to dive at her head. She took a long sea-worn stick from the russet sand and held it above her head so that their aggression would be no threat. A seal stuck its head out of the water twenty yards from shore and swam along beside her as she walked, occasionally disappearing underwater, to reappear a little further along her path. Perhaps this was a sentry.

As she climbed the hill above Glimmerwick, she looked back at the settlement below and saw the bent figure of Lowrie a'Wurlie out walking with Nell. He too was heading for the shore, a poor wizened creature now, like a trow or goblin or some tiny Pict.

To Linda, Lowrie was the representative of a whole world in which his way of life belonged. An old way, where satisfaction grew from very little cultivation. In her teenage years, when the boom was first rumoured, she had disagreed with him on almost every point. Now she was not so sure. What had she gained from oil except a bag of trouble and confusion, an uprooting, compensated by a wad of £20 notes? Or would she have gone this way whatever? She would never know. There are no ifs in life, they are mythical. There is only ever one option, the one which we choose. The others we imagine are but distractions, employed by those who hope to avoid decision. Yet even they choose in their negativity, by allowing life to decide for them. This much she knew.

She reached the top of the hill. To the west, the land ended a hundred yards away in red cliffs. Below her lay another bay to round, that of Hamnavoe. And beyond that, where the shores of the north and the west meet, the Grind o da Navir.

•••

Lowrie saw Linda's distant figure on the hillside, etched black against the skyline. He recognised her, but couldn't straighten up and raise his arm to wave to her. So he carried on down the slope to the field where his prize Shetland sheep and their new-born lambs were grazing. These were the only stock on the croft which Lowrie still took responsibility for.

He sat on a large rock, which had cosseted his bony backside many times before. He patted old Nell on her head; no doubt she was still eager for work, he thought. He could see it in her eyes as she sat panting, watching the flock. But like him, she was too old. He rolled himself a cigarette and looked again to the hill above. Linda's matchstick shape was gone.

"Every year, da voar," he grunted, smiling.

He was thinking about the talk he and Linda had had the night before. Then, she had tried to explain to him how she felt about the Grind o da Navir. He had said nothing, but had listened. She hadn't explained herself well, but he knew what she was talking about. He too had felt the power of the place when he was a young man raking the coast for driftwood.

She had told him too of her notions of the 'time before time', as she put it. This too he had felt for years without speaking out.

When she had said all she wanted, Lowrie shook his head.

"We'll never understand it, Linda," he had said. "Best no wasting time on it."

But he too had not explained himself well. It wasn't that he felt her earnest searching was in vain, only that the kind of secret she was seeking was not the kind which one might discover, like treasure, buried in a larchwood box. It was a secret which was inside, which was better understood than known, which would swell slowly like the tide as life went on, till it filled a body up and so was full itself.

This he had tried to say, but had not the words to express it.

He let these thoughts go then. He was content now to watch. He threw the cigarette end from his hand and turned his eyes to the sea. Something dark on the water caught his sight. He screwed his face up and tried to focus. Was it the shape of a small whale underwater? Certianly it was a colour he had not seen for a long time, for there was no record of it in his memory. And Lowrie knew the colours of the bay of Glimmerwick as well as any native creature. It seemed to be moving inwards to the shore on the tide. Maybe it was a dead whale. He watched closely. Then something else caught his eye, something moving in the heart of the dark shape. What was it? Nell stood up and joined her master in his sentry stance. For a few minutes nothing happened. Then quite suddenly the dog growled and let out a loud howling bark which made the old crofter's bent back straighten.

It was . . . OIL!

A small dark patch lying thin on the water of Glimmerwick, moving towards the shore on the flowing tide. And in the middle of it was a bird of some kind, fluttering desperately as it tried to escape.

Lowrie's heart turned to thunder.

"Filth!" he shouted, "God damned filth!"

•••

Linda stopped. Her eye had fixed on the grass in front of her. She smiled and knelt down, then shrugged the rucksack from her shoulder. She looked around her, scanning the ground carefully. Yes, it was the first of the season. Tiny nippled mushrooms, their heads no bigger than the nail of her pinkie, an oily grey-brown in colour. She laughed to herself, then picked one carefully with the forefinger and thumb of her right hand. Magic mushrooms. She remembered the first time she had tripped, back in 1977, with Eddie Haggerty and a friend of his on what was now the new golf course in the Dale of Lerwick. She'd been a bit reluctant — the things tasted so horrible — a mixture of liquorice and soor milk. But after a few she got used to the taste — then all of a sudden she began to hear voices, a million all at once speaking together, calling out 'We're here, we're over here!'.

And right enough, wherever she went under their instruction, she found little clumps of them. The others thought it was 'amazing'! She was completely in tune with them. After all, it was what they wanted, Haggerty explained to her, to be eaten then spread through shit — had she never wondered why the sheep and cattle were so relaxed?

Linda sat down cross-legged and stared out over the sea towards Glimmerwick on her north-west, hidden by the cliffs and sheltered under the round bulk of Ronas Hill. She popped the nippled head into her mouth, then started picking more to eat. It was such a beautiful day to be out. This coast was so wild and old and hers.

When she reached the Grind o da Navir, it was after twelve o'clock and the sun was at its highest in the sky above. She was hungry and a little tired and her head was buzzing with strangeness. She unpacked her bag and ate a sandwich before entering the temple itself. Then she took her materials and walked down into the rock sculpture. No voices spoke. All she could hear was the rush and rumble of the sea at the cliff foot below.

She started to paint, trying to use her palette to its full potential, mixing colours. The wind kept rising in gusts from the sea below wrinkling the paper. Her first results were disappointing. The light from above was so bright and the reflection off the sea so strong that the rocks appeared to be a uniform red-grey with no detail.

After a number of attempts she stopped and went to fetch more food from her bag, which she had left outside the sacred place. By now she was so absorbed in her own head that she did not think of the voices she had heard before or the power of the place. She took another sandwich and an apple and returned to the rock seat where she had left her materials.

As she ate, she tried to analyse what she was doing wrong. She looked at the seven half-finished sketches, laid them out on the rocks in their evolutionary order, pinned down with small stones. She noticed that the colour became more subdued with each sketch, till the last was almost a grey-red-blue abstract of the shape of the grind itself.

She picked this last attempt up and turned it upside down, on its sides and all round, trying better to understand. She chewed on her sandwich as she did so, utterly absorbed, hardly aware of the effects of the magic mushrooms, expanding and focusing her thoughts.

Holding the bread and cheese in one hand, she turned the sketch over so that she could see through it, holding it up to the sun.

A great wave broke on the cliff foot below, sending a shower of salt spray into the air, some of which carried so high on the force of the swell that it broke into the temple, despite its great elevation.

As the sea water fell around her, splattering the paper, Linda smiled. The ocean's gateway into the land, she thought, looking up the sheer rock walls which formed the grind. And then she understood.

"A grind will open both ways," she murmured, on the threshold, looking at the now wet sketch which was reversed against the sun. Realisation of a strange unconscious kind spread over her.

"Of course! Grinds can open both ways! This is no just a door for the ocean, it's the door out too!" she shouted, her voice ringing round the amphitheatre and back inside her head, echoing loudly from the rock. She stood up: she understood!

This was the doorway, the grind itself. This was the way that the ancients had left and the way they must come back! Through the Grind o da Navir, from the rock of life into the ocean of death, from the ocean of death to the rock of life . . . the gateway: da Grind!

And suddenly, out of the silent rumbling, came a horde of voices crying, more pained and more loudly than ever before, so loud that she was almost deafened.

"Free us," they cried. "Free us!"

Louder and louder, millions of ancient voices, piercing her eardrums till she screamed in terror. The rock temple seemed to spin round about her, faster and faster, till she stumbled and fell, dizzy and breathless. What power was this? What had she tampered with? What had she done?

"Stop!" she cried, but they did not.

"Please!" she cried, but they knew no mercy.

"Freeusfreeusfreeusfreeusfreeusfreeus," they called.

"What must I do?" she shouted, and silence was restored.

One voice, one sweet voice, a voice she knew, said . . .

"JUMP!"

It was her mother, her long dead mother who had killed herself so many years before. Linda's mind and body were no longer her own. She was possessed.

"No," she pleaded.

And then, quite quietly, came the same familiar voice.

"Then you can never know us. We are dead, Linda Watt, and so are people no longer. If you will not join us, another will."

The temple was silent then. Linda's eyes bulged in her head, no longer moonish, now burning. She looked all around her. Slowly the rock ceased moving. Her sea-splattered drawings fluttered in the wind. The sun still glanced its brightness from the ocean below. She looked at her watch: the digital display read 2.22. She had been there two hours yet had touched eternity.

"Mam?"

The sea below rumbled again.

"Mam?"

And the voice came again, quietly. It said . . .

"I dønna hing laek muswubs, sylken, lippenin dy hert's dim riv. Dead fokk's will gings wi dir bairns, lukkin dem as I lukk de t'da places qhuar da blue-mondet stonns'll crø wis. I'm glansin swarmin fleein; licht, dy meed in aa. Daeth vamms nothin, only lowses, slips de fae da lemskit mondi du caas 'life'. Hit's juist a stab athin a sea o wantin, wir spirits most ootgeng be understandin wings!"

The tongue she spoke with was old, containing fragments of the Norn language native in the islands before the coming of the Scottish influence. Linda knew few of the words she had heard — yet she understood. Some part of her which was not her, but a part of her belonging knew it all.

Linda understood. A cloud crossed the path of the sun, throwing a sudden gloom over the ocean. As she raised her eyes she could just make out the distinctive shape of an oil tanker slipping silently beyond the horizon.